HEY JOE

THE UNAUTHORIZED BIOGRAPHY OF THE ROCK CLASSIC

New York Times Best-selling Author
MARC SHAPIRO

For more information contact:
Riverdale Avenue Books
5676 Riverdale Avenue
Riverdale, NY 10471.

www.riverdaleavebooks.com

Design by www.formatting4U.com
Cover by Scott Carpenter

Digital ISBN: ISBN: 978-1-62601-332-2
Print ISBN: 978-1-62601-333-9

First Edition December 2016

TABLE OF CONTENTS

This Book is Dedicated to....

First and foremost this book is for my wife Nancy, who thought this was a good idea. To my daughter, Rachael, who probably won't get this, but eventually she will. To my granddaughter, Lily: Don't be alarmed, Grandpa is always like this. To Brent, Robert and Layla: You'll get used to it. Brady and Fitch (RIP) told me it was cool…whatever it is. My agent Lori Perkins, who probably was not quite sure, but had the courage to say yes, anyway. To all the musicians who made this possible, and to those who were willing to talk about it once they stopped laughing. And finally, to all of those who take this stuff seriously and often suffer the slings and arrows because of it. Don't worry, I have it on good authority that we'll all win out in the end.

And a very special thanks to Camilla Saly-Monzingo, my editor, who fact and double-checked my myriad references and kept me out of trouble.

Acknowledgements

Couldn't Have Done It Without You

Finding musicians who would be willing to talk about *Hey Joe* in any way, shape or form was always going to be the tough nut to crack. Time, memory and mortality limited the gene pool somewhat as I attempted to connect the *Hey Joe* dots across the years and decades. And there were those who, for whatever reason, were not interested or did not want to be involved. That's cool. No arms were twisted in the making of this book. Fortunately, there were some who graciously came forward with their time and memories.

Keith Olsen (The Music Machine): He was easy. Just give him a time and a phone number and he was there. Gave a good account of himself on the specifics of The Music Machine and the song. A big plus was how a band like The Music Machine functioned in the infancy of the Sunset Strip rock and roll scene. If he didn't remember something, he would tell me so. But he remembered a lot.

Rob Landes (Fever Tree): Initially Rob was a bit amused as to why a book on *Hey Joe* and why him? But he warmed to the idea with an insightful chronology of a band that had been up, down and was suddenly hanging by a thread whose only lifeline appeared in the form of a song, *Hey Joe*.

Don Preston (The Mothers of Invention): Easily one of the highlights of my *Hey Joe* research was when Don, in mid-interview, broke into a version of *Hey Joe* on his keyboard, complete with what would turn out to be the first time he ever sang the song. Don is a musicians' musician. That's his vocabulary and he was quite good at describing how Frank Zappa managed to parody *Hey Joe* and turn it into a work of art.

Toody Cole (Death Moon): Calling her cold and making my pitch resulted in sheets of laughter. When she realized I was serious, she proved quite the guide through the regional rock scene of the 80's and 90's and how *Hey Joe* was actually a pivotal point in the band actually making a living. She was still laughing at the end of our conversation.

Randy Holden (The Fender Four, The Sons of Adam, Blue Cheer): Randy has a kind of water off a duck's back attitude. He had been through a lot. He could have been a contender if the music biz fates had been kinder in the 60's, especially as it pertained to The Sons of Adam coming this close to having the first commercial release of *Hey Joe*. He remembered the 60's experience as good even when it wasn't always so. Randy filled in a lot of important spaces in the evolution of *Hey Joe*. Many thanks and keep rocking.

John 'Eddie' Edwards (The Vibrators): Caught Eddie as The Vibrators were pulling into a San Francisco hotel on yet another US tour from one of the oldest and continuously active punk bands on the planet. In between checking into the hotel and preparing for sound check, Eddie gave an insightful look into how *Hey Joe* impacted and influenced the music scene in the UK and how The Vibrators were diligent in beating the shit out of their version of the song. Everything in Eddie's take on *Hey Joe* seemed covered with irony and humor. But why not? Eddie's been around almost as long as *Hey Joe* has and he deserves to tell the tales any way he damned well pleases.

John Medeski (Medeski, Martin & Wood): John was late to the evolution of *Hey Joe*. He discovered Hendrix's version after the fact. But as part of the avant-garde jazz group Medeski, Martin & Wood he would describe his group's foray like an explorer discovering an out of the way plateau. He described *Hey Joe* as light years from calculating yet ripe with new opportunities. John describes his group's journey into *Hey Joe* in often vague, subtle tones. But his efforts are paving the way for what the future holds for the song.

Vernon Reid (Living Color): Vernon was calm, intellectual and serious about what *Hey Joe* has meant on a historical level and what the song portends for the future. It seemed to come by him naturally. He was cerebral in dissecting *Hey Joe*. And as far from boring as he could possibly be.

Otis Taylor: One gets the feeling that Otis Taylor is an artist masquerading as a veteran blues man. Especially when it comes to *Hey Joe*. He talks calmly, almost matter of factly about the love affair he's had with the song over the course of several albums and a myriad of styles. He was easy to talk to. And, perhaps more importantly, to listen to. Because he saw a future for the song and he was glad to be along for the ride.

Addendum

And although they will be thanked by name later in the book, I want to extend my heartfelt thanks to the non-musicians, the producers, family members, managers and those unknowns who were an important cog in the *Hey Joe* pipeline. The people behind the scenes who patiently received and considered my emails and finally agreed to answer my questions and to help push the story of *Hey Joe* further down the road. This is a story that I felt passionate enough about to undertake. I could not have done it without you.

Thanks for all your help. Marc out.

Author's Notes

Are You Nuts?

Before we get started I have a confession to make. I am an addict.

No it's not drugs, alcohol, gambling, or most aspects of daily life that give me the shakes and drive me to distraction. What sets me to Jonesing is the obscure, the fringe stuff, the little known facts that keep me awake nights.

I haven't fallen prey to the stuff that baffles and defines most fanatics. Things like calculating sports statistics bore me to death. And don't try to bend my ears with the latest gluten/vegan concoction guaranteed to make me painlessly lose a ton. Do I live and die by computer games? No. I don't play games. Am I hip to every facet of modern technology? I know just enough to create an international incident.

This is how I roll when it comes to obsession.

I can tell you how many cigarettes actor Forrest Tucker's character smoked in the movie *The Crawling Eye*. Two classic television shows that are most likely classic only to me are *T.H.E. Cat* and *Manimal*. Jewish rock stars? The greatest hit of *The Bubble Puppy*? Hell, on a good day I can even recite chapter and verse on who really killed Lincoln and Kennedy. And yes, it was the same person. If it rates at some importance to me, I'm there. And I can mentally picture most of the civilized world running the other way.

I have the most wonderful wife on the planet, but if I had a dollar for every time a long-winded explanation of mine caused her eyes to glaze over, I'd be a very rich man. The same tolerance or inattention extends to my daughter, who chalks up my blathering to old age and more old age. Hell, even my granddaughter and dog have been known to give me funny looks when I've been on a rant. Bottom line, my insanity or eccentricity has never been in doubt.

Expounding on all things obscure is not for polite society. It is for the denizens of science fiction and horror conventions and for those who find meaning and psychological purpose in the most 'out there' images and topics that populate the dark corners of life.

But my case is a bit different.

I write for a living, which tends to lend itself to some contrary thoughts and attitudes. I once turned a buck by convincing a magazine that they could not continue as a viable literary entity if they did not have a story about rock stars who died on stage while performing. I once turned a couple of side questions to a roadie who used to work for Led Zeppelin into a conversation about the time he worked for Apple Records, and the result was cash on the barrelhead, his eyewitness account of John Lennon and Yoko Ono fighting, and his divulgence of heretofore unknown details about the tour Lennon was planning when he was shot and killed.

But those were small potatoes. It would take my mania for all things *Hey Joe* to expand my tolerance for obscurity and turn it into this real live book. The reasoning behind this sudden mania for a song that is essentially about premeditated murder came late into my world. I grew up with the song as presented on *93 KHJ* and *1110 KRLA* by The Leaves. The song was mildly gnarly, and, by the standards of most teenage sensibilities, it registered as both cool and dangerous. For a long time that was pretty much the extent of my attraction and obsession.

That was until not too long ago, when I came across a website devoted entirely to the song *Hey Joe*. It was a revelation. There were others out there like me, and they had not been locked up. And boy this was the beginning of a brave new world. It turns out that close to 1800 covers of the titular song existed, and a lot of them were by pretty big names, many of whom had experienced *Hey Joe* in their misspent youth, and survived the encounter on the road to stardom. And those were only the versions that received marginal release. There's this guy in France named Christian Arnould, who also lives and breathes *Hey Joe*, to the extent that he has made it his life's work to dig up the most obscure international *Hey Joe* 45's, bootlegs and everything else on the planet. His contributions alone bumped my list of *Hey Joe* covers to well over 2000 and counting.

Adding to my mania is the fact that, to this day, nobody is completely sure who actually wrote the song.

Everybody and his mother has taken credit for writing *Hey Joe*, including a Scottish balladeer, a UK pop group named Marmalade and the British metal band Deep Purple. The contrariness and the inconsistencies were maddening. Who could possibly care, let alone lay down money, for something that had little or no potential for big time success?

I would. But then I wasn't in my right mind at the time.

The idea bubbled under as I worked on various other projects. But it resurfaced late in 2014 when my agent and I were bouncing ideas off each other. If you're familiar with my bibliography you know that the notion of writing an entire tome on the little known and little cared for intricacies of one song seems a little far-fetched. But I had worked up a lot of sweat equity over the years, and my instincts tend to be more spot on than not. So when the discussion came around to whether we should do a book on John Lennon's women (a long percolating project that may, one day, still happen), I took the plunge and enthusiastically pitched the alternative idea that would ultimately become *Hey Joe: The Unauthorized Biography of A Rock Classic*, thinking all the while that my agent's eyes would glaze over in that non-commercial stare and we would move onto the next and much saner project.

Boy, was I surprised when her response was, "Do either the Lennon book or the *Hey Joe* book." And it was my decision to make. Shortly after picking myself up off the floor, I sat contemplating my decision. The Lennon book would be fun. But the *Hey Joe* book would be insanely fun. Ten minutes after being given the option, I was on the horn with my decision that it would be *Hey Joe*.

Much to her credit, my agent did not back down. It would be *Hey Joe*.

Writing the book was a rollercoaster ride. There were literally hundreds, if not thousands of cool musicians, producers and, yes, seeming non-entities, to talk to—that is if they wanted to revisit *Hey Joe*. Some were obviously long dead, or short on memory. Many of my requests went unanswered, some responded with their memories in due course, and a couple came through within minutes. A couple of noted authors on the subject of 60's music, who will be profusely thanked and noted elsewhere in the book, volunteered contact numbers and their notes from their books that pertained to the song.

When it came to drawing as complete and as critical a picture of a simple song and its impact on the world, my research was diligent to the point of madness.

I have a love/hate relationship with technology, but I have to admit that, when it came to searching out the myriad of versions of *Hey Joe*, the Internet was aces. I easily listened to a couple of hundred different versions of *Hey Joe*. I found my *Hey Joe* senses were sharpest in the morning. The sounds of *Hey Joe* at 6:00 a.m. were not uncommon. If you don't believe me, just ask my neighbors. By noon things started to get a bit fuzzy. Anytime after 6:00 in the evening…well how do you spell blotto? I was hearing *Hey Joe* in my dreams. The heavyweight, name versions were there, but so were a ton of obscure ones, many of which were quite good. There were some unexpected surprises, too.

And I'm not going to lie to you. Some of the versions of *Hey Joe* were only average or competent. Others were sub-par, and still others were uninspiring barkers. Everybody has an opinion. I tended to end up on the side of the good stuff, but I urge you, if you truly want to follow me down the rabbit hole of *Hey Joe*, feel free to listen far and wide and form your own opinion.

Not surprisingly, a lot of people laughed their asses off when I told them what I was doing. Some musicians got a chuckle at the idea that *Hey Joe* was worthy of a book, but then they got into the spirit of fleshing out their experiences with the song. One musician happened to be sitting at his keyboard during our interview and broke into an impromptu rendition of the song. It was the first time he had sung it after decades. It doesn't get any cooler than that.

I went into the interviews with no expectations or agendas. I considered anybody who agreed to do them a serious bonus. My opening shot was, "Tell me the first time you heard *Hey Joe*." Then, in a journalistic sense, we were off and running.

The result was a lot of labor intensive but loving work that now results in *Hey Joe: The Unauthorized Biography a Rock Classic.* This book is my Christmas present to those who are willing to risk delving into surreal waters and literal tidal waves of WTF, perhaps to emerge with a newfound respect and understanding for people a lot like me.

Like I said. I am addicted. There is no cure. But who in their right mind would want one?

Marc Shapiro
2016

Introduction

Remember The Time?

I heard a lot of music back in 1966. Transistor radios were the hip conduit when out and about. The sound quality varied depending on where you were, or how you twisted the flimsy antenna. But one thing you could always count on was music and lots of it.

It was the time in Sothern California of *KRLA*, *KHJ* and numerous other Top 40 rock stations. Radio jocks like Dave Hull, Sam Riddle and The 'Real' Don Steele piloted the airwaves with hip between-song patter, lame jokes and outrageous sound effects. But most of all it was about the music.

Rock and pop were in flower in 1966, thanks in no small part to the coming British Invasion, and the music de jour was rarely over two minutes and 20 seconds of pop, slightly dusted, with clangy guitar and nasal teen-friendly vocals. These songs were the heartbeat of the 60's generation's restless youth. Surf music had seemingly been the first strike against lame pop, which was slowly fading into the sunset. Being considered hip and cool meant listening to *Misirlou* by Dick Dale and The Del Tones, *Nut Rocker* by B. Bumble and The Stingers and *The Bristol Stomp* by

The Dovells. The Top 40 list that was that in name only. The reality was that there was a Top Ten list that was played over and over on a seemingly continuous loop between jock talk and the quick snippets of news.

In an hour you might hear your current favorite three times, just long enough to be able to sing along with it and, by weeks' end, be sick of it. At its zenith, Top 40 songs were built for the short haul, with even a smash hit likely to have a life expectancy of a few weeks. New additions to that vaunted inner circle of ten would magically appear on a weekly basis.

It was the ideal universe of an easily distracted teen: effortlessly digested, danceable bits of cotton candy with rarely a hint of controversy and just plain outrage.

Then something unexpected happened in May 1966: something called *Hey Joe* by a Southern California band called The Leaves.

Musically the song was cool, serviceable pop, a solid guitar riff backed by crisp backbeat, a subtle bass bottom and an all-together radio friendly vibe. On the surface, *Hey Joe* was party music. You could dance to it, bob your head to it, and, in a fairly innocent way, show how cool you were. But then there were those lyrics, those oh-so-unexpected, damnable oh-so-not friendly lyrics. Lyrics that would be added to, subtracted from and made just plain different in so many ways in the decades to come.

What follows is the original, registered lyrics to *Hey Joe* dated January 12, 1962, registered in the name of singer/songwriter Billy Roberts from the files of the *Library of Congress* and posted, among other places, on the *Hey Joe Versions.com* website.

Hey Joe, where you goin' with that money in your hand?

Hey Joe, where you goin' with that money in your hand?

Chasin' my woman, she run off with another man.

Goin' downtown, buy me a .44.

Goin' downtown, buy me a .44.

When I get through, that woman won't run no more.

Hey Joe, what are you gonna do?

Hey Joe, what are you gonna do?

Take my pistol, and kill her before I'm through.

Hey Joe, I heard you shot your woman dead.

Hey Joe, I heard you shot your woman dead.

Yes I did, got both of them lying in that bed.

Hey Joe, where do you think you'll go?

Hey Joe, do you think you'll go?

Leaving here, think I'll go to Mexico.

Yes, I'm going, going where a man can be free.

Yes I'm going where a man can be free.

'cause ain't no hangman gonna put no noose on me.

Just like that, premeditated murder to a rock and roll beat was coming out of transistors and car radios as kids made their way in the world. And it gets a whole lot grimmer.

Through the song's fast, safe as mother's milk rocking tempo, *Hey Joe* not only shoots his old lady, but runs on down to Mexico where he deftly avoids the hangman's noose and lives happily ever after. At the time, *Hey Joe* was considered a catchy pop song. But once the song faded into the either, it was on to the next, and with teen attention spans being what they are, nobody seemed to give the violent lyrics much thought—at least not initially.

Hey Joe was not around long enough for many to truly dissect it. Within a matter of weeks it was up and down both the Southern California charts, where it did actually sit at Number one for a nanosecond, and the national charts, topping out at a fair to middlin' Number 31, and then off to obscurity.

In a recent conversation, Dave Hull "The Hullabalooer," one of the top jocks at *KRLA* when *Hey Joe* came and went in Los Angeles, stated that "It has been 50 years since that song was on the charts, and I don't remember anything about it." But when pressed, Hull did acknowledge, "I was working at *KRLA* in 1966 when *Hey Joe* was on our playlist. But, to be perfectly honest, the song did not last there at all. In fact, *Hey Joe* by The Leaves didn't make it into the top 30 nationally that year, and since *KRLA* was prone to dropping songs that didn't appeal to a large share of the audience, we would have dropped them pretty quick, as we did in this case."

A follow up single by The Leaves, *Too Many People*, was slightly brash, but not as alarmingly high strung as *Hey Joe*. It did not do as well, and just like that, The Leaves were history.

Or were they?

A certain outrageously cool aura, the low-slung fog and the bad cold that would not go away, seemed to linger around *Hey Joe*. People who cared about such things would constantly return to it, marveling at how a song so literally extolling the virtues and rewards of murder could seep through to public awareness on the wings of lightweight pop. The lyrics and their presentation would ultimately stake out the claim of *Hey Joe* as being something special—as well as a bit sinister and unsettling.

There was a pulpy rawness to it all. Something direct and almost matter of fact in the song's delivery. It was primitive stuff, all eye for an eye, on a level that would get into kids' heads as they waited for the next zit commercial. Bottom line, it was a goddamned great song that would appeal to a whole lot of people for decades to come.

In those early days of psychedelia and the Sunset Strip, a lot of musicians who were just beginning to find their way were also discovering the possibilities of *Hey Joe*.

Paul Rogers, legendary singer from Free and Bad Company, acknowledged in an interview with *Rock Cellar Magazine* that the first time he heard *Hey Joe*, it scarred him for life in the best possible way. "The first time I heard *Hey Joe* it blew my mind, and it still does today. Whenever I hear that song it takes me back to that day when I first heard it. That was an amazing moment for me."

Musicians could instinctively see the hipness and attitude of *Hey Joe*. At a time when 60's hippie culture was beginning to have its day, most any band with a record deal or a club gig saw fit to work out *Hey Joe*, either as album filler or as a legitimate album cut. Bands such as The Standells, Love, The Music Machine, The Byrds and Fever Tree worked the song to varying degrees. Some totally went rock crazy, all fuzzed out and raging. Some decided to up the horror, teen angst and dour elements that were far removed from the original's tone. Still others literally returned to their roots, seeing the bluesy tradition of the downtrodden and ultimately redeemed between the grooves, and went quite earthy with the song.

As the decades progressed, *Hey Joe* was quite literally the song that would not die.

Cher had a minor hit with it. Wilson Pickett also hit the charts with a particularly smoldering version of the song. Along the way, Jimi Hendrix recorded what many consider the definitive version of the song *Hey Joe.* The metal band Deep Purple included a decidedly Euro-rock version of *Hey Joe* on their debut album. Robert Plant's pre-Led Zeppelin band, *Band of Joy*, also recorded a version. Years later Led Zeppelin would record and perform their own version of *Hey Joe* for a Hendrix tribute album. And in what would, to many, become the stamp of legitimacy for *Hey Joe*, Bob Dylan, in a secret session with Jimi Hendrix band member Noel Redding, would record the song.

Many observers of the evolving pop music scene would often marvel at how a blip on the radar by, essentially, a one-hit wonder could be carrying so much emotional and creative weight. But the reality was that one could walk into just about any club in the mid-60s and hear a band plying their *Hey Joe* trade. Some better than others, but the telling point was that everybody was doing it.

Historically speaking, *Hey Joe* would permanently cement itself in rock and roll lore at the Woodstock Festival. The final day's festivities concluded with Hendrix's legendary rendition of *The Star Spangled Banner* that ended the set. But as literally thousands of concertgoers made their way to the exits, a roar went up from the crowd. They wanted an encore and they were not to be denied. Ever the considerate performers, The Jimi Hendrix Experience shambled back on stage and literally played the final song of The Woodstock Festival…

…*Hey Joe*.

In the years following the release of *Hey Joe* in 1966, music scholars also began taking a liking to the song, revisiting it in both scholarly and, well, rock and roll ways.

Among these was noted gonzo rock critic Lester Bangs, who acknowledged in an excerpt printed in *HeyJoeVersions.com* that, "For a few years in the 60's everybody and his brother not only recorded *Hey Joe* but also claimed to have written it. It was an easy song to play because of its catchy, continuous chord progression, not to mention the machismo of its text." Author and rock music historian Dave Marsh also acknowledged the importance of *Hey Joe* in another excerpt in *HeyJoeVersions.com,* stating, "The song probably fits the academic definition of the folk process better than any rock and roll song."

Record producer and manager Ted Fox (Buckwheat Zydeco) was growing up on the East Coast during that first real wave of *Hey Joe* mania, and remembered it clearly during a 2016 interview with the author. "Growing up in the 60's, every single high school band played *Hey Joe*. You had to play *Hey Joe*.

Hey Joe was the cool song at the time. For me, it was kind of like *My Generation* and *Louie Louie*. It was easy to play and if you were, like, a 14 and 16-year-old teenage kid from the suburbs, singing a song about shooting your woman and taking off for Mexico...well that wasn't *Chapel Of Love. Hey Joe* was some kind of nasty, underground business whose lyric quality had great appeal to teenage white kids."

Over the decades *Hey Joe* would become a rock and roll perennial that would leave itself open and available to any style of music. In a creative sense, it was easy access. Everybody could do it and they did. It seemed like everybody at the time had primitive recording equipment and the blueprint for at least local success, and could record a single, or, if really ambitious, an EP. The song that came and went in Los Angeles in the 60's was now everywhere on the planet.

By January 2015 it was reported that more than 2000 versions of *Hey Joe* had been recorded by both famous and obscure groups alike, thus cementing its reputation as a legitimate classic. It had, some years previous, been anointed by *Rolling Stone's* The 500 Greatest Songs of All Time list with a robust ranking of Number 201. But at the end of the day, it's been the loyalty and reverence of the fans and music lovers that kept *Hey Joe* alive into the 2000's and has catapulted the song into the record books.

On May 1, 2006, 1,572 guitarists, a mixture of pros and rank amateurs, gathered in the town square of Wroclaw, Poland to celebrate *Hey Joe* with a massive, monster jam that immediately qualified for inclusion in *The Guinness Book of World Records*. The notoriety quickly turned into an annual event in Wroclaw. On

May 1, 2007, 1,881 guitarists kicked out the jams to *Hey Joe* once again and broke the Guinness record. May 1, 2008 saw 1,951 join in to yet another record-breaking *Hey Joe* explosion of sonic celebration. Six thousand three hundred forty-six returned on May 1, 2009 to break the record one more time. By 2012, the *Hey Joe* Jam had turned into a fairly regular event and was drawing guitar players from literally every corner of the planet. This time the record was broken yet again as 7,273 players paid homage to the legendary song.

Hey Joe was now culturally, socially and musically iconic. These tribal gatherings had become something joyous, personal and psychologically satisfying.

It would be a joy that would be played out during the 2012 *Hey Joe* jam when, amid the cacophony and chaos that was an homage to the song, one excited player exclaimed to *Guitarworld.com*:

"Are you sure you can hear me? I think I'm getting lost in the mix."

Chapter One

Who Wrote *Hey Joe*?

This is a tough one. Who wrote *Hey Joe*? Everybody who came in contact with the song seemed to have an opinion or a theory.

Folksinger Tim Rose, who championed the notion that *Hey Joe* came from traditional origins, swore up and down in an interview on the television show *Later... With Joolz Holland* that *Hey Joe* was based on a long-lost Appalachian ballad. Jimi Hendrix, whose version of *Hey Joe* is considered by most critics and fans to be the definitive take, claimed in liner notes on his collection *Jimi Hendrix: The Ultimate Experience* that *Hey Joe* was actually a 100 year-old cowboy song.

These are all great stories, but, ultimately, they are just stories. There is much in the historical record to indicate that *Hey Joe* did in fact rise from a family tree that regularly mixed music with violence.

Hey Joe in its original format was a very simple blues-based configuration: simple chord progressions and a simple question and answer lyrical take. For all intents and purposes, *Hey Joe* has always been perceived as an original song conceived out of the mind of a songwriter in and around the mid-50's named Billy Roberts. But there is much to indicate that that version of *Hey Joe* may have owed more than a bit of its creation to a couple of songs that came first.

The earliest manifestation of the *Hey Joe* theme was the song *Little Sadie,* which, in itself, is a mystery. To this day nobody is certain who wrote *Little Sadie,* although many have stepped forward to take credit for it. There have been reports that black prison chain gangs in the late 1800's would sing *Little Sadie* out on the dusty roads while swinging their hammers.

More diligent research done in a series of articles by the magazine *No Depression* indicate that *Little Sadie* which, like *Hey Joe*, has murky origins as to who actually wrote the song, seems to have taken its origins from an actual crime, possibly African-American related, that took place in either Texas or Mississippi. *Little Sadie* was your classic underground mystery at first, a regional song, not recorded, that reportedly became a favorite among wandering musicians who performed in shantytowns, dive bars and anywhere they could earn a dollar. It is known that *Little Sadie* had interpretive legs, moving through the years, easily refined and reimagined in racial and economic tropes by countless musicians of all races.

What is known for certain is that the song *Little Sadie* has gone by a lengthy list of alternative titles including *Bad Lee Brown*, *Bad Man Ballad*, *Cocaine Blues*, *Transfusion Blues*, *Late One Night* and *Penitentiary Blues*. What most researchers do agree upon is that Clarence Ashley released the first recorded version of *Little Sadie* in 1930 on the *Rough Ways* label. A look at the lyrics, while presenting a somewhat different scenario, immediately strikes one as distinctly similar to the modern day notion of *Hey Joe*.

> *Last night I was makin' my rounds*
> *Met my old woman and I blowed her down*
> *I went home to go to bed*
> *Put my old cannon right under my head*
> *Judge says murder in the first degree*
> *I say Oh Lord have mercy on me*
> *Old Judge White picks up his pen*
> *Says you'll never kill no woman again*

This lyrical fragment, taken from the 1948 publication *Ozark Folksongs Vol. II*, seems to indicate that the notion of murder of women and its consequences has been around a long time. It has existed so long, in fact, that modern artists such as Johnny Cash, Bob Dylan and The Grateful Dead would make the song part of their regular live set list, primarily as envisioned by this Clarence Ashley version.

The *No Depression* article also disclosed another song as a touchstone for *Hey Joe* that had a much clearer true-crime origin. On the surface, *Stagger Lee* was conceived as a simple revenge tale of one man shooting another to death for trying to steal his hat. The reality was that on Christmas night in 1895 a local pimp named 'Stag' Lee Shelton was having a drink in a saloon with an equally hair trigger underworld type named Billy Lyons when the pair got into a drunken argument, during which Lyons grabbed Shelton's hat off his head. Shelton responded by pulling a gun, shooting Lyons, retrieving his hat and leaving the saloon. The law of the underworld, especially as it pertained to the pimp culture of the day, acknowledged that the killing was justified. But the long arm of the law felt differently.

A year later, Shelton was tried and convicted of Lyons' murder. But by that time, one Professor Charlie Lee, according to an 1897 *Kansas City Newspaper* article, had penned the story in song called *Stagger Lee*. The song would outlive its real-life origin and be embraced by jazz and blues musicians, ultimately gaining a sense of legitimacy in 1959 when it became a chart-topping Number One hit by country singer Lloyd Price.

Yet another song in the *Hey Joe* family tree and, yes, also based on a true crime, was the dark and dusty revenge ditty entitled *Frankie and Albert*. The *No Depression* article states that in October 1899, Frankie Baker discovered that her much younger boyfriend Allen Britt had won a local dance contest with another girl. Reportedly an argument ensued that resulted in Baker pulling a gun and shooting Allen. Baker was ultimately acquitted of the shooting on the grounds of self-defense. In the spirit of cashing in, a musician named Bill Dooley wrote a song entitled *Frankie Killed Allen*. The song would be a gold mine for Dooley, published and recorded dozens of times over the years by the likes of Jimmie Rogers and jazz greats Louis Armstrong and Count Basie, and under such alternative titles as *Frankie Killed Allen* and the more identifiable *Frankie and Johnny*.

Jerry Hopkins, renowned author of such rock and roll tomes as *The Jimi Hendrix Experience*, *Elvis: A*

Biography and *No One Here Gets Out Alive* (with Danny Sugerman) recalled in a 2016 interview with this author that his first reaction to hearing *Hey Joe* by The Leaves was that its roots ran deep but in a much different direction. "It [the song] reminded me of a much earlier one, *Frankie & Johnny*, which used the same angry lover's plotline, though in *Frankie & Johnny* it was the woman who shot the man. That song was from a much earlier era. Mae West did a version of *Frankie & Johnny* in 1933 and Guy Lombardo recorded the song in 1947. So it's possible that *Hey Joe* could have been an answer tune to *Frankie & Johnny*."

The first song to actually go out under the title of *Hey Joe* would be a 1953 country hit by singer Carl Smith. While using *Hey Joe* as the title, and adopting the question and answer lyrical format would become a trademark of modern versions of the song, this *Hey Joe* took a more well-mannered look at love lost, and only at the end, when a friend decides to move in on his territory, does the narrator indicate that there just might be violence in his now former friend's future. Given the erratic nature of the music business at the time, Smith's *Hey Joe* would be the first song with that title to go Number One on the country charts.

The next stop in this odyssey is the mid-1950's and a folksinger named Billy Roberts, and this is what most historians cite as the true beginning of the 'who wrote *Hey Joe*' controversy.

Billy Roberts (born August 16, 1936 in Greenville, South Carolina) seemed destined for the straight life as a student in the famed Military College of South Carolina. But a long simmering love for music, and the growing folk music scene of the mid-50's, finally won out. Roberts dropped out of Military College, picked up a guitar and a harmonica (as a guitarist he long maintained he had been mentored by blues great Sonny Terry), learned some songs and followed the wave of itinerant and hopeful musicians to New York's Greenwich Village where he soaked up the brewing social and musical revolution, busking on the streets and plying his trade in area coffeehouses.

Along the way, Billy Roberts found love...and a whole lot more.

Niela Miller, an aspiring singer/songwriter, had, likewise, taken her aspirations to the East Coast. Miller was pretty much a performer of the times, evoking love and emotions lost and found as well as occasional dark, personal drama. She would have a minor success along the way. Her song, *Mean World Blues*, would, ultimately be recorded by Dave Von Ronk and, in 1961, she would appear onstage at the Indian Neck Folk Festival in Branford, Connecticut, opposite the likes of Bob Dylan and Connie Francis. But, for the most part, Miller was primarily a part of a struggling group of folksingers, attempting to make their way busking and landing the odd club gig. But Miller's niche in folk music history would be cemented when she came across Billy Roberts and fell in love.

On the website *Hey Joe Versions* she recalled how she met Roberts. "Billy Roberts was my boyfriend in the late 50's. He and I met when he first arrived in town, and we were both going into an event at Gerde's Folk City. He had no place to stay, so naturally I invited him to stay with me, and one thing led to another."

With the deepening relationship Miller felt comfortable sharing her songs with Roberts, who would listen for hours as she played and ultimately taught him how to play all of her songs. One was called *Baby, Please Don't Go To Town*. The relationship between Miller and Roberts would eventually cool, and the pair went their separate ways, but apparently the basic song structure and the question and answer lyrical idea of *Baby, Please Don't Go To Town* would continue to stick in Robert's head.

Roberts' travels eventually took him out of the United States and to Scotland, where he made the acquaintance of a local singer named Len Partridge. Partridge, in conversation with *The Independent* in 2003, disclosed that he had worked with Roberts on the song *Hey Joe* in endless jam sessions in 1956, and, as was the custom in those freewheeling creative exchanges of the day, would embellish the song according to his own tastes and attitudes. Partridge conceded in conversation with *The Independent*, "Don't even ask me now which bits were added by me. I can't claim credit for it [*Hey Joe*]. That really has to go to Bill." However, Partridges' denial of ownership of the song would not deter the later notion that *Hey Joe's* roots were actually in traditional music lore. One outlandish allegation, for a time, had the song dating back several hundred years. It was an allegation that has carried little weight and has never been proven.

Adding yet another layer of confusion/mystery to the origin of *Hey Joe* was a memory of Roberts' friend Darrell Jenkins who, in *Hey Joe Versions*, recalled that Roberts had told him that he wrote *Hey Joe* in 1959. "I don't know how accurate that is," Jenkins qualified, "but it is what he told me."

The truth behind the mystery of who wrote *Hey Joe* operated in limbo for several years. In the folk and coffee house circuit *Hey Joe* was being passed around, and became a staple for a number of singers. Roberts would reportedly play the song live on a regular basis, but, as was often typical in those early halcyon days of popular music, the singer had been a bit naïve when it came to doing things like copyrighting his songs. Consequently, the song was essentially in the public domain. It was obvious that others in the close-knit folk community had been playing the song, and nobody had taken the time to legally make it their own.

Roberts, whose dealings were often blinded by generosity, made a grievous error. The singer had been a solid performer and quite good at networking and schmoozing other performers. He would occasionally show up on the undercard of performances by A-list performers. In the early 60's he was on the bill at San Quentin Prison with headliners Johnny Cash, Louis Armstrong and Sarah Vaughn. Among the appreciative and truly captive audience was a prisoner reportedly doing one-to-ten for drug charges. His name was Chet Powers.

Chet Powers, who also went under the names Dino Valenti and Jesse Orris Farrow, was an often brilliant singer/songwriter whose career had been regularly sidetracked by drugs. Powers, whose two claims to fame would become writing the classic hippie ode *Get Together* and, as Dino Valenti, fronting the 60's San Francisco band Quicksilver Messenger Service, somehow made contact with Roberts, and a quick and mutual friendship developed. Power's downward slide had resulted in his having to sell the rights to the song *Get Together* to pay for what would be an unsuccessful legal defense, and at that time he was hoping for an early release, if he could prove he would have some form of income upon release from prison.

The particulars of the transaction between Roberts and Valenti are unknown. Speculation has deepened on the question of whether any money changed hands, or if what they were doing was actually legal, seeing as how Roberts, in the eyes of the law, did not legally own *Hey Joe*. But the upshot was that Roberts signed over the rights to *Hey Joe* to Valenti, and thus Valenti would soon be a free man.

Roberts thought little of the favor and went about his business, playing the coffee house and club circuit, and occasionally opening in concert venues. In a memory that appeared in *Hey Joe Versions*, Barbara Porter Salls recalled a partying couple of weeks in Paris, in which she hung out with Roberts and his, at that time, traveling buddy Dino Valenti. The pair made quite a stir busking on Paris streets and singing *Hey Joe*. Former Roberts producer and manager Hillel Resner recalled in a piece for *Popsickle* that Roberts had recorded a tape of songs in 1961 in which he sang *Hey Joe,* but said that the tape was never released.

As has been previously noted, Roberts was an outgoing guy who seemed to make friends just about everywhere he went. One such stopover was in Washington D.C. in 1962. Roberts found enough regular coffee house gigs to keep him in the area for two years, during which time he made the acquaintance of a George Washington University student named Mike Rivers. Rivers, recalled in a 2015 email interview that during an informal hang with Roberts he had been the one to record Roberts singing a number of songs including *Hey Joe.* It was this tape, he claimed that went on to be passed around and ultimately made its way to Resner. "I have an informal recording of Bill which includes *Hey Joe* that I made at *WGRW* (the *George Washington University* radio station). There was no date on the recording but I believe it was 1962," he said.

Rivers also acknowledged that around the time of the recording, Roberts sensed that he had something special in *Hey Joe* and that, in a legal sense, it was time to cover his creative ass.

"My participation in helping Bill copyright the song *Hey Joe* was picking him up at the Library of Congress and giving him a ride back to his apartment in Washington D.C." recalled Rivers. "He said that he found quite a few songs with the title *Hey Joe* with copyrights registered, but none were the same as his so he went ahead and did the paperwork."

Perhaps Rivers was giving Roberts too much credit for having the business savvy necessary to copyright his song. At least that was the opinion of an obscure folksinger named Neil Lewis who joined the ever expanding back and forth on *Hey Joe Versions* when he related a meeting with Roberts some years later in which the topic of conversation was the legal side of *Hey Joe.* "We discussed the whole *Hey Joe* mess, and he gave full credit to a guy named Howie Mitchell in D.C. who insisted that any of us who were writing tunes should send a copy to ourselves, registered mail and keep it, unopened, as proof of when we had written it. Billy said this was what substantiated his claim."

For all intents and purposes *Hey Joe* was now legally noted as 'written by Billy Roberts.' But legality was an often elusive beast, especially when it came to the music business. And so, sometime after Roberts made *Hey Joe* his, Niela Miller came back into his life, and, as she stated, stirring the pot in *Hey Joe Versions*, she was not happy.

"Imagine my surprise when I heard *Hey Joe* by Billy Roberts," she said. "There was my tune, my chord progression, my question/answer format. He dropped the bridge that was in my song and changed it enough so that the copyright did not protect me from his plagiarism."

Word of the *Hey Joe* controversy would make its way through the folk community. Musicians and songwriters were taking a second listen to Miller's *Baby, Please Don't Go To Town* and Robert's *Hey Joe* and were choosing up sides. Many loyalists insisted that Roberts had, indeed, ripped Miller off, while others stood steadfast in the fact that the chord progressions and question/answer lyrical format were derivative of many different styles and open to varying degrees of interpretation (i.e. plagiarism). At one point, famed folksinger and social activist Pete Seeger stepped forward and offered to speak on Miller's behalf if she decided to pursue the matter in the courts.

"But I decided not to go through with all the complications of dealing with him [Roberts]," she reflected. "He never contacted me about it or gave me any credit. He knows he committed a morally reprehensible act. He never was man enough to make amends and apologize to me, or to give credit for the inspiration. Dealing with all that was also why I made the decision not to become a professional songwriter. It left a bad taste in my mouth."

But perhaps the most unusual witness would step forward in 2008. The controversy over *Hey Joe* had caught fire on the *Hey Joe Versions* website, and anybody with even one degree of separation was stepping forward to add credence or to muddy the mystery even more. In this case, it was Andrew Christopher Roberts Jr., the son of Billy Roberts. Andrew claimed he had been born in 1961, around the time his parents were divorcing, and though he would not meet his father until 15 years later, he maintained adamantly that while his father may have been a lot of things, his father was not a crook. By this assertion, he gave passing credence to the theory put forward by Jerry Hopkins. "The chick who claims that Bill stole *Hey Joe* from her is wrong!" he insisted. "The song was written as a parody to the old song *Frankie and Johnny* and he had my mother on his mind! So we can put that nonsense to rest once and for all!"

Or can we?

Over the years, the aforementioned Tim Rose, whose reputation for stretching or distorting the truth was right up there with his musical talent, would continue to float yet other and often borderline outrageous versions of how he had written *Hey Joe*. And his stories would inevitably introduce yet another character to the mystery.

One story would introduce a semi-familiar name. Vince Martin.

Martin had been a minor blip on the music scene, scoring a Top Ten hit in 1956 with the song *Cindy Oh Cindy* backed by the group The Tarriers. Martin would strike out on his own and, in the ensuing years, become a journeyman folksinger as a solo performer, and, most notably, as a duo with the much better known singer/songwriter Fred Neil. In an in depth look at the song *Hey Joe* in *No Depression Magazine*, Martin muddied the waters a bit more when he offered that he had picked up the song *Hey Joe* from Valenti sometime in the early 60's.

Not surprisingly Rose would enter the picture with yet another variation on the 'who wrote *Hey Joe*?' mystery. In a quote from the *No Depression* piece, Rose stated in 1997 that Martin and he were performing at The Flick Club in Coral Gables, Florida. When…

"I was working at the same club as Vince Martin and he was singing two verses of it [*Hey Joe*]. I said 'that's an interesting song. I mean not much to it but did you write that?' He said 'No that's all I know of it. I think that it's an old Appalachian tune.' I said 'Do you mind if I take it and maybe do something with it?' He said 'Go ahead.' So, I did."

Rose's continuing stories of how it was he who had written *Hey Joe* would occasionally pick up a supporter. Jake Holmes would swear up and down in an interview with *Perfect Sound Forever.com* that it was indeed Rose who had written the song. It should be noted in advance that Holmes' version has been contradicted in several points, but are included here in an attempt to paint as balanced a portrait of the controversy as it played out at the time.

"I was in a band with Tim called Tim Rose and The Thoms (a/k/a The Feldmans) in the early 60's," recalled Holmes, "and I have to give Tim the credit. He was the one who came up with that thing that Jimi Hendrix did later, *Hey Joe*. Our idea with Tim and The Thoms was to take folk songs and turn them into rock songs. Tim had this friend [Billy Roberts] who had written this folk song called *Hey Joe*, and Tim took the song and rearranged it for us to play. We were the first band to play it. A few other bands picked it up later. But Hendrix would hear Tim do *Hey Joe* in England a few years later. That's where he got it and used it, and that's how Tim got ripped off."

Rose turned *Hey Joe* into a slower, much more raw and tension-filled song that was in line with his vocal timbre. To the extent that once Rose inked a deal with Columbia and the single of *Hey Joe* was released in May 14, 1966, Rose's version was credited as 'Arranged and Adapted by Tim Rose.' It was hardly airtight proof that Rose had actually written the song, but rather had simply tinkered with it. Long story short, Rose's version of *Hey Joe* would be a regional hit but nothing more, and would be a distant memory, thanks, in large part, to a third attempt at *Hey Joe* by a Southern California garage band called The Leaves. But ever the opportunist, Rose managed to parlay his alleged authorship of *Hey Joe* into the music world's flavor of the moment during the remainder of the decade, and into a fair amount of critical praise. He suddenly had higher-profiled appearances in rock arenas: an example being a three-day gig opening for The Grateful Dead at The Fillmore December 9-11, 1966. Rose was not trotting out *Hey Joe* as his reason for fame, but if asked he would dutifully offer up his version of how he came to author *Hey Joe* (a version that could change at the drop of a hat), and seemed perfectly content to let lawyers ultimately decide who wrote the song.

No matter who was having or not having success in the early 60's with *Hey Joe*, the consensus was beginning to coalesce around the fact that Billy Roberts seemed to have the street cred, if not traditionalist support, that he had, indeed, written *Hey Joe*.

Chapter Two

Win, Place and *Joe*

Randy Holden would be the first to tell you that his memory of the 60's often runs up against the brick wall that is being 71. But the good natured guitarist whose resume includes stints in the early 60's favorites The Fender Four, Sons of Adam, and, for a brief time, what was once considered the loudest band in the land, Blue Cheer, is quick to point out certain things are crystal clear. Namely the early days of the Sunset Strip music scene, which is what greeted The Fender Four when they arrived fresh faced from Baltimore in 1964.

"When we first came out to L.A. there really was no music scene on the Sunset Strip," he related to this author in 2016. "At that time, it was basically Trini Lopez and a lot of Las Vegas kind of acts. The music had not really broken yet. The first thing of any consequence going on at the time was surf music."

He also remembers his introduction to a bit of music mayhem called *Hey Joe,* which, as he recalled, was barely a blip on the screen when The Fender Four arrived on the scene. "I know we never heard it on the radio because, to my knowledge, it had not been recorded by anybody, and was not on the radio. I remember hearing it live by the group Love, and we also heard The Leaves do it. I know it was always a story that every band on the Sunset Strip was playing it at one point, but the fact was we were among the very few that was playing it when we first came out here."

The Fender Four quickly became one of the must-see bands during those early days on the Strip. The result was that in short order in 1964 they were on stage in some club almost every night of the week. Holden recalled that it was during those exciting rock and roll days that *Hey Joe* entered their musical space. "We started doing *Hey Joe* out of happenstance and necessity. We didn't really have a set list, and a lot of nights we were doing five-hour sets. We just started playing it [*Hey Joe*] one night, and there was a power to it, and so we just decided to put it in our set."

It was about the time The Fender Four were discovering *Hey Joe* that Imperial Records was discovering them, and the result was a series of surf-oriented singles that came and went without a whole lot of notoriety. "During the Imperial Records days there was never any inclination to record *Hey Joe*. At the time surf music was still real big, and we were doing surf music, to a large extent. After a time, we began adding more and more vocals to what we were doing, and *Hey Joe* became a regular part of what we did."

Things were beginning to change in 1965. "I remember Kim Fowley and a group of Sherwood Forest-looking people came backstage at one of our shows. Kim said, 'Your name is shit. You should change it.'. So we came up with the name *Sons of*

Adam. That was the year we were the opening act for The Rolling Stones in Long Beach, CA, and we were playing *Hey Joe* at that point."

Sons of Adam was also beginning to draw a lot of interest from record labels, most of which Holden remembered with a jaundiced eye. "At the time ,we were getting all kinds of offers. Most of them were bullshit. Everybody wanted us, but we felt they were offering nothing in return."

The band finally signed a limited six-month contract with *Decca Records* in 1965. Wasting no time, *Sons of Adam* immediately went into the studio with producer Gary Usher, with an eye toward getting enough material together to put out a series of singles. Holden, acknowledging his bias, offered, "Those were the best recordings we had ever done. We were playing extraordinarily well live, at that point."

But Holden recalls that there was one glitch in the process that centered around *Hey Joe*. "We did have a disagreement during the recording of *Hey Joe*. One of the other guys in the band wanted to sing *Hey Joe,* but he really didn't sing it that well. He didn't do it to my taste, and I felt I could do it better. I probably should have put my foot down, but I didn't."

With the sessions complete, the *Sons of Adam* suddenly found themselves in an unexpected *Hey Joe* logjam. As it turned out, Decca suddenly had three acts who had recorded the song. The Safaris, who had already established a large commercial following with a series of well-received surf songs, and a fairly new singer named Terry Knight (who would later morph into Terry Knight and The Pack and, much later, the behind the scenes impresario for Grand Funk Railroad). But the competition did not dissuade *Sons of Adam* from pushing real hard to be the first *Hey Joe* out of the box.

"We had it in our heads that we were going to put out *Hey Joe* and *Mr. You're A Better Man Than I* on the same single. But we were realistic enough to know that The Safaris were considered the fair-haired band at Decca at the time. But from what I understood, the decision makers in New York were pushing Terry Knight. To be honest, Terry Knight's version of *Hey Joe* was not very good."

At the end of the day, Decca decided to put The Safari's version out first. "Our producer Gary Usher was pushing Decca real hard to release our version, but Decca still wanted to release Terry Knight's version. I think it all boiled down to whichever act the label had the most invested in."

In the book *The California Sound: An Insider's Story* by Stephen McPharland, producer Gary Usher adamantly stated, "Compared to The Safaris, the Sons of Adam were total professionals. There was actually no comparison. The Sons of Adam could play the hell out of their instruments, and they were tight and loud."

Although The Sons of Adam would ultimately release three other singles on the Decca label, none of them would contain *Hey Joe*. Holden claims he held out hope for some time that their version of the song would at least show up as a B-side. "I never knew it wasn't being released. I always trusted these guys to do what had to be done. At that time we all felt that getting *Hey Joe* out was what we needed to put us over the top."

Ironically, their version of *Hey Joe* would never be released, and some 50 years later we have only Holden's admittedly biased opinion of just how good their version was. "At the time, I thought it was really good. The only shortcoming was the vocals, which were okay, even though I felt I could have done a really good job. We had the power and the energy on that song. I thought we had done a really kickass job on it."

Holden seemed all right with the cards that were dealt, but in his numerous post *Sons of Adam* musical ventures he has steadfastly refused, in any way, shape or form, to attempt *Hey Joe* again. He puts his reluctance down to a version of *Hey Joe* that would come down the pike two years later. "For me, Hendrix was the definitive version—the way it was supposed to be done. I didn't think it was appropriate for me to pursue the song the way it was formally done by Hendrix. I felt he dominated that song."

Finally, Holden remains nonplussed that Sons of Adam might have become part of history if the fates had been kinder and their version of *Hey Joe*, had been the first to be released. "I've been on the cusp a few times. The kind of success that *Hey Joe* might have brought is the only thing I really wanted for years, and I've worked my ass off for it. *Hey Joe* is kind of the epitome of what's been going on for a long time."

Chapter Three

Hitting The Strip

If Billy Roberts had seemingly walked away winning the "Who authored *Hey Joe*" battle, other elements were conspiring that would ultimately have Roberts at least temporarily losing the war.

Dino Valenti was not one to look a gift horse in the mouth. Not long after Roberts gave the ownership rights to *Hey Joe* to the singer so he could appear solvent and get out of jail, Valenti took it upon himself, shortly after moving to Los Angeles, to register his own copyright for *Hey Joe*, listing himself as the writer, with Third Story Music agreeing to publish the song under Valenti's name.

As it turned out, Valenti had a motive in moving to Los Angeles. The music scene was evolving into a vibrant mix of pop, rock, folk and a new offshoot called psychedelic. Bands were springing up on every street corner, and some of the earliest of those were becoming stars along a suddenly revitalized stretch of Hollywood's Sunset Strip. There were opportunities everywhere, and Valenti was in town to both land a gig, and to hawk his newly registered *Hey Joe* to any and all takers.

Valenti quickly made his way into the Hollywood rock community, landing the occasional solo gig in the many clubs that had suddenly sprung up in the area. Perhaps most importantly, he was spreading the gospel and potential of *Hey Joe* to anyone who would listen.

The early 60's was a fast-paced lifestyle that, for the bands at the time, meant recording albums and the all-important singles in days and hours, often literally between gigs, and getting out as much new music as possible as quickly as possible. This meant that new songs were often at a premium, and groups often turned to remakes of established songs or non-band songs "with a kick" to fill out albums. Among those earliest groups showing interest in *Hey Joe* were what was considered the cream of the crop of the first wave of Sunset Strip bands: The Byrds, The Leaves, The Surfaris, The Standells, Love and The Music Machine.

Hey Joe was met with enthusiasm from a lot of sources, and the unspoken race to be the first to officially record the song would provide its own set of intrigues, and no small amount of controversy. Valenti had become particularly tight with David Crosby, then a recent addition to the fledgling lineup of The Byrds. They were, at the time, a regular fixture at the club Ciro's. Crosby had enthusiastically embraced *Hey Joe* and during their early five-sets-a-nightclub gigs, and the band would regularly find a place for *Hey Joe* in their set. Crosby's lead vocals on the live version of *Hey Joe* were the perfect complement to their sound, ultimately raw and plaintive, which most importantly rang true to the song's intent. But there was a slight problem as The Byrds began prepping for the recording of their first album, *Mr. Tambourine Man.*

Author John Einarson, whose book *Mr. Tambourine Man*, *The Life And Legacy of The Byrd's Gene Clark* is, in many quarters, considered the definitive look at the life and times of the band, spent a lot of time with the band's first manager, the late Jim Dickson, who recalled going a couple of rounds with Crosby over *Hey Joe*.

"At the time, I still had control over everything [with the band], and one of the things that I didn't like that they did live was David's *Hey Joe*. He did it well, and the audience liked it, but I didn't think a song about a guy who shot his girlfriend and was running away to Mexico was proper for The Byrds [first album]." But Crosby insisted and, consequently, turned the recording of the band's first album, *Mr. Tambourine Man* into a nearly knock-down drag-out fight. As Dickson explained, "At one point I sat on David's chest and pinned his shoulders down, because David did not want to put a vocal on the song *Chimes of Freedom*, the last song on the first album."

Eventually Dickson, along with pressure from the rest of the band, won out, and Crosby would lay down the vocals, but he would continue to fume. When it was time for The Byrds to return to the studio some months later to record their follow up album *Turn! Turn! Turn!*, the battle of wills between Crosby and Dickson once again centered on whether or not to include *Hey Joe*. "At the time, he just didn't grasp the feel of The Byrds," related Dickson.

With The Byrds' sudden stardom a shakeup in management and producers followed, and, recalled Dickson, the band decided they could manage themselves. Dickson was shown the proverbial door.

He insisted in his conversation with Einarson that, "One of the reasons David engineered my getting thrown out was because I would not let *Hey Joe* be on the *Turn! Turn! Turn!* album."

Crosby would ultimately win the *Hey Joe* battle when, with Dickson out of the picture, the band agreed to throw Crosby a bone, and their rendition of *Hey Joe,* with his vocals, appeared on The Byrds' third album *Fifth Dimension. Fifth Dimension* was an uneven album at best, in which the road-weary band channeled their personal and creative differences into a wide array of songs and styles, and, true to Dickson's prediction, *Hey Joe* seemed out of step with what The Byrds were doing. According to Dickson, Crosby was man enough to admit it. "He [Crosby] eventually did it, but afterwards would come to me and admit he had been wrong."

"It was a mistake," admitted Crosby in the book *The Byrds: Timeless Flight* by Johnny Rogan. "I shouldn't have done it. Everybody makes mistakes."

In hindsight, many felt that Crosby's *Hey Joe* was a solid song and a standout on the album. Crosby's bandmate Chris Hillman, in comments in *The Byrds Lyric Page.com*, was unabashedly supportive of the tune, and of Crosby. "I think David did it [*Hey Joe*] really good. I think I don't take it as seriously because The Leaves, who were kind of a Byrds' clone, had already put it out. It was one of David's songs that he always did with the band. He brought it into the studio and we worked it out, electrically."

The Byrds would continue to play *Hey Joe* live throughout 1966 and '67, and, most notably, during their appearance at the groundbreaking Monterey Pop

Festival. The Leaves, who had been in the audience several times to hear it in those early days at Ciro's, eventually took the hint.

Throughout the early to mid-60's the Sunset Strip, and the bands who plied their trade in the clubs, had become a literal Wild Wild West when it came to the song *Hey Joe*. Nobody knew for certain who really wrote it (although many did not press the issue when Valenti claimed he had), and so even the most obscure bands were quick to claim ownership. Ultimately it was The Leaves who got the first bit of commercial success out of the song.

The Leaves were a Southern California garage band that had received some local Los Angeles club and concert scene fame with their own brand of rock and pop with an edge, typified by the likes of their woefully underappreciated single, *Too Many People*. However, the group had national ambitions on their mind, and figured *Hey Joe* might be that ticket to ride.

The Leaves were nothing if not perfectionists, and the band did not want to burn any bridges in the process. Despite the fact that Valenti , in most circles, was considered the de facto writer, the band went to The Byrds, and specifically to Crosby, for permission to record *Hey Joe*, given that the story going around was that The Byrds were reportedly getting ready to release their own version. Crosby gave The Leaves his blessing and a clear pathway to being the first band on the Southern California scene to record and release *Hey Joe*.

Around this period one could throw a rock through any club door on the Sunset Strip and hear *Hey Joe*. According to The Leaves' Jim Pons in conversation with

60'sgaragebands.com, the song had become a staple. "Everybody seemed to have their own version of that song in Hollywood in those days. We just added it to our set like everyone else. But we added an instrumental break in the middle that no one else had. I think it might have given our version some commercial potential."

For his part, The Leaves' John Beck was feeling a deep sense of propriety, and perhaps a sense of paranoia which he described in a quote from the book *Sixties Rock: Garage, Psychedelic and Other Satisfactions*. "What happened was some of the other bands started getting wise to the song and doing it, and then I heard that the band Cory Wells and The Enemies were going to record the song, and that really pissed me off because they weren't entitled to it at all. We were smart enough to know that whoever put the song out first was going to have a hit with it."

Feeling the pressure, the band literally raced into the studio and recorded what they felt was a satisfactory first version of the song. *Hey Joe* by The Leaves was released in November 1965 but was quickly pulled because of what the band deemed poor sound quality. Adding further confusion to the who wrote *Hey Joe* mystery, the publishing arm of The Leaves' record label decided it was in everybody's best interest to copyright *Hey Joe's* words and music and attribute them to Beck. A second version of the song was released in early 1966 and flopped. But The Leaves were determined to get it right, and turned to another up and coming Los Angeles band for help.

Love, who at the time were going by the name The Grassroots, had been toying with the song *Hey Joe* in their live shows since September 1965.

According to author Jerry Hopkins who at the time was managing the band, they had recorded a trio of demo songs which may have included *Hey Joe*. When former The Byrds roadie and emerging guitarist Bryan MacLean joined The Grassroots and introduced the song to the band, their mercurial leader Arthur Lee latched onto it and turned it into an electric, full-speed-ahead rock and roll showstopper.

As often happened in this close-knit 60's music community, everybody knew everybody else. This six degrees of *Hey Joe* resulted in Leaves' member Bob Lee ringing up Grassroots' member Johnny Echols with a request. In his detailed, definitive biography of Love entitled *My Little Red Book: Love Day By Day: 1945-1971*, author Bruno Ceriotti added another layer to the *Hey Joe* authorship conundrum when he interviewed Johnny Echols.

"What happened was Bob Lee from The Leaves, who were friends of ours, asked me for the words to *Hey Joe*. I told him I would have the words the next day. I decided to write totally different lyrics. The words you hear on their record are ones I wrote as a joke. The original words to *Hey Joe* are 'Hey Joe, where you going with that money in your hand? Well I'm going downtown to buy me a blue steel .44. When I catch up with that woman, she won't be running round no more.' It never says 'Hey Joe where you goin' with that gun in your hand.' Those were the words I wrote just because I knew they were going to try and cover the song before we released it. That was kind of a dirty trick that I played on The Leaves, which turned out to be the words that everybody uses."

Echols was not the only one to play around with

the song's lyrics. The version of *Hey Joe that* The Leaves released in November 1965 featured the line 'Think I'll go down to where the grass roots grow.'"

Bottom line: the third time was the charm for The Leaves' version of *Hey Joe*. The song would go Number One for a millisecond in Los Angeles, and Number 31 nationally. Unfortunately, the album that contained the song did not fare as well. Five weeks at a slow crawl on the Billboard charts saw 'The Leaves *Hey Joe*' manage no higher than 127. But to those who would ultimately care about such things, the first recorded version of *Hey Joe* was a marginal hit.

But was it really the first?

The story going around during the time of The Leaves' release, and one that was duly postulated by author Michael Hicks in his book *Sixties Rock: Garage, Psychedelic and Other Satisfactions*, was that The Surfaris, a surf group whose big hit of the day was *Wipeout*, had recorded *Hey Joe* as the B-side of an obscure single called *So Get Out*, reportedly released late in 1965. Music lore suggested that The Surfaris, in deference to David Crosby, had decided to delay the release of the single until The Byrds had recorded their version. Consequently, The Surfari's version of *Hey Joe*, which had reportedly been recorded in September 1965, had originally been slated to be on their album *It Ain't Me Babe* in November 1965. While die-hard conspiracy theorists have continued to insist that The Surfari's version came first, the prevailing theory (based on a Decca Records release schedule and the personal archives of Gary Usher who produced The Safari's single) was that the song was released in either May or June 1966, and faded away with little interest or notice.

Ultimately, it would be the notoriety surrounding The Leaves version that would trigger the first recognized legal battle over *Hey Joe*.

Hillel Resner met Billy Roberts in Reno, Nevada in the winter of 1961-62. They became fast friends (a friendship that would have Resner managing Roberts for a period of time). During this time Roberts, as was his wont when meeting new people, played Resner all of his songs, including *Hey Joe*. Resner recalled in a commentary on the website *Hey Joe Versions,* that at one point in that initial meeting Roberts produced a registered copyright on *Hey Joe* dated 1962. Flash forward to 1965 when Roberts and Resner hooked up again.

"Billy returned to San Francisco in 1965, and around that time I happened to hear The Leaves recording of *Hey Joe* at a friend's house in North Beach. I immediately called Billy on the phone and asked him if he had heard it. He had not. Billy was furious since he owned the first copyright to the song. As it happened my father was a well-known attorney in San Francisco, and I introduced Billy to him."

Resner's dad did his due diligence, tracking down the song's publisher, Third Story Music, and the company's top dog Martin 'Mutt' Cohen, who informed Robert's attorney that Dino Valenti had claimed to have written the song, and that Third Story Music published it with Valenti listed as its writer. When the attorney produced Robert's much earlier copyright registration, Cohen knew he was backed into a corner, and quickly removed Valenti from any ownership of *Hey Joe*. Of course, as Resner would recall in *Hey Joe Versions*, the publishing company set conditions for making the change.

Marc Shapiro

"Third Story agreed to recognize Billy's authorship, providing that he give them a share of the songwriter's royalties in perpetuity."

Third Story Music's outrageous and highly unethical request was, sadly, not uncommon in the music business in the 60's, or just about any time, for that matter, but it was a small price to pay to officially get Robert's name beyond reproach as the author of *Hey Joe*. Not that Roberts did not harbor some resentment at what he considered Third Story's rip off. Years later Roberts released his one and only album, *Thoughts of California*, which was conspicuous by the absence of *Hey Joe*. Resner would speculate that excluding the song from the album was the singer's way of avoiding paying any royalties on the song *Hey Joe* to Third Story.

While Roberts officially began collecting royalties starting in 1966, Valenti, in the meantime, had been spreading the seeds of *Hey Joe* in several directions for some time.. For the record, The Leaves version was credited to Dino Valenti. *The Grassroots* had eventually changed their name to Love and recorded their version of *Hey Joe,* credited to Valenti, in January 1966 for their debut album entitled *Love,* which would be released in April 1966. Love's version was lyrically and musically all over the place, with new and traditional lyrics mixing with the band's patented lighting fast brand of psychedelia.

Hopkins also happened to be Love's very first manager, and, as such, had a front row seat for the band's earliest performances of the song. "I thought the band's version of *Hey Joe* was one of their most popular songs on the club circuit," he told the author.

40

"My association with the band, all bias aside, probably gives the band's rendition a huge emotional edge. Arthur Lee (Love's singer) was a mean motherfucker."

And here's where things get kind of interesting. Depending on how purists want to look at the whole 'who came first' in regards to *Hey Joe*, a dark horse emerged in the most unlikely of studios: a Hollywood apartment bedroom. An amazing quasi-rewrite of *Hey Joe* under the title *Wanted Dead or Alive*, credited to a group called The Rogues. Given the vagueness of release dates, it may well have been the first recorded version of *Hey Joe,* although with an obvious asterisk.

The Rogues were two 'out there' minds named Michael Lloyd and Shaun Harris (who would later go on to form the equally 'out there' West Coast Pop Art Experimental Band), under the stern supervision of then relatively new kid on the scene, future music renaissance man Kim Fowley. In a 2009 discourse on a website called *Opulent Conceptions* between a blogger named Colin and an in-the -know person named Tom, the intricacies of this *Hey Joe* became clear:

"This amazing, slow rewrite of *Hey Joe* was recorded in a Hollywood bedroom in 1965 while The Byrds and The Leaves were on the air with the original *Hey Joe.* Kim's inspiration was to keep the chords and feel of the original song, adding new lyrics and making it a sequel. Shaun Harris handled the vocals while Michael Lloyd kept time drumming with his knuckles on the floor."

The reality was that it would be 1966 before either of those groups recorded their versions, which, in essence, makes The Rogues' version the first, albeit again with that non-purist asterisk.

The Rogues' version would get only sporadic release beginning in the late 60's and primarily overseas, and the reality remained that *The Leaves'* version would get the lion's share of the credit for getting *Hey Jo*e rolling on the Sunset Strip.

Another Los Angeles band of note, The Standells, turned in a pop, yet snarling version of *Hey Joe,* that turned up as track six on their album *Dirty Water* in 1966. That version was credited to Chester Powers (Dino Valenti's real name). One story that made the rounds was that The Buffalo Springfield, while never actually recording the song, played it regularly at early Los Angeles club gigs. However, the early experiments into *Hey Joe* were not limited to Los Angeles and the Sunset Strip bands. A missing link hailed from Pittsburgh and went under the moniker of The Swamp Rats.

On the surface, The Swamp Rats were no better or worse than the myriad of garage bands that were sprouting up like weeds in the wake of the Leaves' success, but their interpretation prefigured a later genre of music. Their bread and butter, not surprisingly, consisted of covers. And like most teen bands of the day, they lasted a nanosecond (the non-scientific equivalent of a year and a half). But on the strength of a handful of singles and largely forgettable—unless you were there—live shows and teen dances, *The Swamp Rats* created a hybrid genre of music: proto-punk. It was punk intensity and attitude, that pre-dated the punk rock movement.

The Swamp Rats' biggest hit was a single that featured *Hey Joe* as the B-side to an A-side cover of *Louie Louie*. The Swamp Rats' version of *Hey Joe* was

2:08 of sneering, angry vocals over a buzzsaw musical backing. It moved at a pace that most modern-day punk bands would envy. The Swamp Rats were short lived, but they were definitely a sonic vision of things to come.

Easily the most intriguing version of *Hey Joe* would come from The Music Machine, a band powered by striking baroque vocals and slightly schizoid psychedelic instrumentation. At their most inward-looking, lyrically they were right up there with The Doors as an alternative to the reigning pop style.

Like most bands of this period, The Music Machine had one legitimate hit in *Talk Talk* and a couple of bubbling-unders during a lightning fast two year run, before dissolving in a spray of management, band member and label problems. But along the way there was *Hey Joe*.

Original Music Machine member Keith Olsen related in a 2015 interview that the band was literally working 24/7, following *Talk Talk*. "In those days, we were always touring and making appearances on the music television shows. We had what amounted to a pretty regular gig on the Dick Clark show, *Where the Action Is*. We were asked to do the top hits of the day and then lip-synch them on the show.

"We would literally do a *Where the Action Is* and then jump in a van. Then we'd go into the studio, sometimes all night, and record a bunch of new material, because in those days you always had to get new songs out there real fast for *Where the Action Is*. We ended up doing so many covers and we'd have to do them quick, while they were still on the charts. That's how we ended up picking *Hey Joe*."

43

Olsen remembered being somewhat impressed the first time he heard *Hey Joe*. "Everybody was doing it at that time, so it was hard to remember which version I had heard first. It had to be Love's version or The Leaves. My reaction was that it was a cool song. I know there was something raw and kind of angry about it. It wasn't like most of the songs you were hearing on the radio in those days. Let's face it, there weren't a lot of songs about a guy killing his old lady and then running off to Mexico on the radio in the 60's."

Olsen admitted that he was not too specific about the details of the recording the song, except that, like just about everything else surrounding the band at that time, it was done in a hurry.

"It seemed like we were always on the road," he related, "and we had just come off a 30-day tour and we were beat. But when *Talk Talk* became a hit, the record company immediately wanted a full album out there, which was our debut album *Turn On! The Music Machine*. I know that Sean [lead singer and primary songwriter Sean Bonniwell] was always writing, and so songs were not a problem. But the record label not only said we had to rush the album out for Christmas, but that at least four of the songs had to be covers. The band was not happy about the covers we were told to do, but everybody kind of liked the vibe of *Hey Joe*."

And so one night, after yet another television appearance to flog *Talk Talk*, The Music Machine went to a local studio, and in a space of six hours recorded six songs, including *Hey Joe*. The only thing Olsen remembered about that session is that everything was seemingly done in one or two takes with a minimum of overdubs. He did relate that the haunting, slow and very dark tone of their version was not only the first slow version of the song, but easily one of the most effecting.

Olsen laughingly recalled that back in the 60's The Music Machine was doing what was known as 'double headers.' "We would be the opening act in one city, throw all our gear in a van and race like crazy to close the show 150 miles away.

"I don't remember what time we finished in the studio. But we immediately had to jump into our van and drive about five hours up north to open up a show for The Leaves (with the Jefferson Airplane second billed). When we got there and we were putting together our song list and thought it would be fun to add our version of *Hey Joe* to the set. So we went on and played our set and everything was fine, but when we got off stage a couple of members of The Leaves came up to us and they were really mad. They didn't like that we had played their hit, and now they were going to have to come on and play *Hey Joe* after us.

"The Leaves were yelling at us, saying that we played their hit. They went on stage and let the entire crowd know that we were assholes. But we didn't care because by that time we were already back in the van and on the way to Bakersfield to close another show."

In an interview with author/historian Richie Unterberger, Bonniwell claimed to have heard early slow versions of *Hey Joe* at various points by the folk group The Big Three and Tim Rose, prior to the formation of The Music Machine, adding that the band's state of exhaustion after coming off the aforementioned 30-day tour and putting in long hours on *Where the Action Is* definitely contributed to the distinctive sound of their version of *Hey Joe*.

"We tried to arrange the song in a different way," acknowledged Olsen. "Since Love's version was the one that we heard, we took the song and said, 'Let's cut the tempo.'"

"There was a definite foggy timbre to *Hey Joe* because my voice was exhausted," said Bonniwell. "But it also put a nuance to the song that it probably needed."

Olsen acknowledged that continuing to churn out covers for *Where the Action Is* was, creatively, starting to get on the band's nerves. "We had just finished recording *Cherry Cherry* the day before, and the consensus was [with *Hey Joe*] 'Thank God! We finally had a song that had some kind of vibe to it.' We had just finished recording *Where the Action Is* for the day, we drove to the studio and cut *Hey Joe* in about four hours, we did all the overdubs, mixed the song and were on the bus going back to do *Where the Action Is* the next morning."

Olsen recalled that the songs recorded for *Where the Action Is*, including *Hey Joe*, were never intended to end up on their debut album. "We cut all these tracks and our manager said, 'Well, you've got all these tracks, just use them on the album.' We weren't in a position to be spending $10,000 cutting all new tracks, and so *Turn On* ended up being about a third covers, including *Hey Joe*."

Turn On! The Music Machine was released on December 31, 1966. An initial single peaked at No. 66 on the Billboard charts. By this time the members of the band were fully behind the notion of *Hey Joe* as the follow up single. But growing tensions between management and the record label were now at an all-time high. Bonniwell was incensed. Always a competitive cat, he knew their version of *Hey Joe* had 'hit' written all over it.

But more importantly, Bonniwell also knew that there was this hot young guitarist named Jimi Hendrix who was about to release his version of *Hey Joe,* and word along the music grapevine was that it was going to be a monster.

Chapter Four

Hey Jimi *Hey Joe*

It would be two years (1968) before The Music Machine's version of *Hey Joe* was released by the band's original label, almost as an afterthought. By that time, the original Music Machine had disbanded. Bonniwell had taken the name and a group of faceless sidemen to another label, and was on to other things. As a result, nobody seemed too interested, and *Hey Joe* essentially went unnoticed. Or so it seemed.

Point of fact: by 1966 Hey Joe had become fully entrenched in the rock psyche, often by word of mouth, or because of the perceived cool-factor of the Leaves' version, as more and more musicians discovered the song and were beginning to put their fingerprints all over it. But with this second phase of *Hey Joe* came a second wave of controversy, largely centering on Tim Rose's refusal to give up the ghost when it came to his long-standing flogging of his 'ownership' of *Hey Joe.*

Rose's version of *Hey Joe*, the failed single in 1966 that would appear on his 1967 album *Tim Rose*, had given him a higher profile than pre-*Hey Joe,* and he was more than willing to ride it for all it was worth. Despite the fact that popular opinion had finally settled on Billy Roberts as the author of *Hey Joe*, Rose continued to trumpet himself as the author going so far as to list himself as the writer of *Hey Joe* on both the single and the album. Possibly in desperation, during an interview with *Acoustic Guitar Videos*, he did a sudden right turn in his telling of the tale, and proclaimed that he had heard what he termed "a traditional" version of the song growing up as a child in Florida. This was the very place where he had also claimed he had heard only a fragment of the song as sung by Vince Martin.

From 1962-64, Rose was part of a folk-rock trio called The Big Three (which included future member of The Mamas and The Papas Cass Elliott and James Hendricks (no, not that James Hendrix) who would regularly include *Hey Joe* in their live performances, but never recorded the song. Rose continued to ply his trade on the club circuit, and eventually made his way to the east coast where *Hey Joe* became a regular part of his set at places like The Café Au Go Go, The Cheetah Club and the hip place where only the biggest names played, the East Village club Café Wha?. Also regular at Café Wha? were Jimmy James and The Blue Flames, led by a flashy, wild-looking guitarist, who had been a rhythm and blues sideman with The Isley Brothers and Little Richard. His name was Jimi Hendrix. Hendrix, who later changed the "Jimmy" to "Jimi," would reportedly see Rose perform *Hey Joe* on several occasions, and was quite familiar with the song. Reportedly, he would play around with the song in his highly experimental blues/freak-out style during many of his Café Wha? gigs.

But while there seemed to be no doubt that Hendrix took his earliest *Hey Joe* cues from his days at Café

Wha? and that he had seen Rose perform the song. Rose, in an interview with Ptolemaic Terrascope.com, insisted on yelling fire when there was not even smoke, insisting that Chas Chandler, who would become Hendrix's manager, was actually the one who, upon hearing Rose's version of the song, had suggested it to Hendrix.

"That story is absolutely true," recalled Rose, "and that's not just from me. You can read anything on Hendrix and Jimi always admitted it. When I met him for the first time, the first thing he said was 'Thanks for *Hey Joe.*' I saw him at The Speakeasy Club when I was promoting my song *Morning Dew* in London and he already had *Hey Joe* out, so he was introduced to me and the first thing he did was thank me. I said 'You're welcome,' gritting my teeth, thinking 'You're making millions and I'm not.' But he did acknowledge it and it was acknowledged in books about him. Literally he and Chas Chandler bought the record and listened to it. Hendrix put his own style into it but they almost did the same arrangement, putting Hendrixisms in it."

Hendrix also recalled his brief meeting with Rose in a 1967 *Unit magazine* interview. But he saw that moment a bit differently. "I seen Tim Rose one time in The Village for about half a second when we were on tour in the States. He tapped me on the shoulder and said 'Hi. I'm Tim Rose.' And then he disappears. That's all I've ever seen of him."

Unlike Rose's slight of hand regarding his alleged authorship of *Hey Joe*, Hendrix made no bones about the fact that he had nothing to do with writing the song. But at least one eyewitness would attest to his earliest attempts at playing a 'different' *Hey Joe in the key of Hendrix.*

Randy California, the late guitarist for the progressive rock band Spirit, recalled in a *Straight Ahead* interview that Hendrix was already playing *Hey Joe* very early in his Jimmy James days, during a short time when a very young Randy California was in the band. California said that he had been the recipient of a private backstage lesson on the titular song. "I remember him [Jimi] showing me the chords to play for *Hey Joe* because I had never heard that song before."

Regular attendees at Café Wha? were hip to the fact that *Hey Joe* had quickly become the centerpiece of the band's set.

California acknowledged in the book *The Ultimate Hendrix: An Illustrated Encyclopedia of Live Concerts and Sessions*, "We were mostly doing cover stuff like *Hey Joe*. And since we were doing five sets a night, we used to jam a lot and *Hey Joe* was the perfect song for jamming." In the same book, musician Bob Kulick, whose group at the time, Random Blues, would often open for Hendrix in the club, also recalled that, "He was definitely doing *Hey Joe* as a part of his regular set."

Word on Hendrix was that he was a definite up and comer, despite an outrageous and just plain 'out there' playing and performing style. The crowds were reportedly around the block when Jimmy James and The Blue Flames performed. Among those in attendance was Linda Keith, who was then the girlfriend of The Rolling Stone's Keith Richards, but became Hendrix's afterward.

In a conversation with *The Observer*, Keith remembered the first time she heard Hendrix play *Hey Joe* at The Café Wha?. "You'd come out of the bright sun into this cave of a room. Then the stage lights would come up and there would be Jimi, playing the opening chords of *Hey Joe*. It was quite mind blowing."

Keith would become a regular at Café Wha? when Hendrix would play, and 'mind blowing' quickly became an understatement.

Keith was amazed at Hendrix's talent, and immediately took it upon herself to use her connections to bring him to the attention of the music industry. Her efforts resulted in a tape of Hendrix doing *Hey Joe* finding its way to the UK and to the desk of Chas Chandler, a former musician in the band The Animals, who had turned his attention to managing and producing.

In an obituary that would appear in *The Independent* some years later, it was recalled that Chandler was so impressed with what he heard on tape that he immediately flew to The States and found himself in an audience at Café Wha?, where he would find himself even more impressed with Hendrix's combination of talent and charisma.

In a detailed look at Hendrix's first months in London, author/journalist Jas Obrecht said that Chandler was blown away, in particular, by Hendrix's version of *Hey Joe*. "Jimi was just an explosive kid whose potential struck me," Chandler recalled in the book *Jimi Hendrix Sessions*. "His version of *Hey Joe* really impressed me."

New Music Express journalist Keith Altham, as chronicled in *The Guardian*, would sometime later recall the moment when Chandler heard Hendrix do *Hey Joe* for the first time as something magical. "It was a song that Chas knew would be a hit if only he could find the right person to play it. There he was, this incredible man, playing a wild version of that very song. It was like an epiphany to Chas. It was meant to be."

Former *Animals* roadie Tappy Wright had tagged along with Chandler that night, but had to be won over. "To be honest, I wasn't too impressed at first," Wright said in *The Guardian*, "but when he started playing with his teeth and behind his head, it was obvious that here was something different."

More to the point, Hendrix's smoldering, truly volcanic rendition of *Hey Joe* would seal the deal for Chandler, who immediately offered Hendrix the chance to come to London and become a star.

The nuts and bolts of how Chandler orchestrated the creation of The Jimi Hendrix Experience have been well documented in several books, most notably Jerry Hopkins' The Jimi Hendrix Experience. Obrecht's article indicated that Experience bassist Noel Redding passed his audition to join the band based on his acing a *Hey Joe* rendition. But what has rarely been noted was that Hendrix may have found his *Hey Joe* mojo not so much at the feet of Tim Rose, Love, The Byrds or The Leaves, but rather in the influence of a relatively unknown group called Creation.

Shortly after arriving in London, Chandler and Hendrix had the occasion to take in a Creation show, and what Hendrix most certainly found in Creation's rendition of *Hey Joe* was that creative umph that meshed with his own style.

Creation was a hybrid of sorts, a beat group with the requisite chops needed to ride out the second or perhaps even third wave of the British resurrection of rock and roll. They had, along the way, evolved into a muscular heavy rock band, largely on the mettle of their guitarist Eddie Phillips, a totally underappreciated talent who, rumor had it, invented the style of playing guitar with a bow well before Jimmy Page did, and once turned down an offer to join The Who, but declined in favor of staying with Creation. Their take on *Hey Joe* in a live setting was guitar heavy, with elongated riffs and a sense of threat, angst and danger that may have struck a chord with Hendrix.

Unfortunately for Creation, it would be another year before the release of their 1967 album *We Are Painterman* which contained *Hey Joe,* and would provide a sense of where Hendrix, even on a subconscious level, may have found his musical inspiration for his version of the song. Admittedly, whether Hendrix nicked Creation's version of *Hey Joe* was a relatively minor issue back in the day. But for a small but diehard group of music conspiracy theorists, the issue and the inherent, albeit minor controversy, has continued.

As recently as 2014, "Which came first: Creation or Hendrix*?"* was a major topic of conversation and examination in *OnTheFlipside.blogspot.com.* The website was evenhanded, pointing out that Creation's version had, indeed, been on an album (*Painterman*) that had been released long after Hendrix's *Hey Joe* take, and only in the Netherlands, Sweden, Germany and France. The *On The Flipside* look was inclined to acknowledge that Hendrix did take a number of musical cues from the Creation version of *Hey Joe,* and that certain musical and lyrical twists (most notably a mid-song dramatic monologue in the Creation version) seemed to indicate that Creation were not aware that a Hendrix version existed.

Finally the question was seemingly solved when an interviewer for the enterprising *The Rock and Roll Archives.com* tracked down Creation guitarist Phillips some years later and flat out asked him. Phillips played diplomat when he responded, "We both just liked the song, and we played it in our own way."

During his early days in London, Chandler was taking his charge around to meet some of the top musicians on the scene, and, as the vibe permitted, to sit in with them on informal jams. It was during an informal musical sit-down with Brian Auger's Trinity that Hendrix, for the first time in a remotely informal setting, literally blew the creative roof off of *Hey Joe*. Brian Auger, as related in the Obrecht piece, recalled that Hendrix walked into the rehearsal studio, turned all the dials on a Marshall Amplifiers to 10, plugged in his guitar and, musically, laid waste to *Hey Joe*.

"Everyone's jaw literally dropped to the floor," recalled Auger. "Jimi wasn't following anyone. He was playing something new."

Chandler was taking mental notes. Any doubts that he may have had about *Hey Joe* as the kick starter to his young charge's career and stardom quickly vanished. And as with everything else in the music industry, he knew that speed was of the essence.

Chandler wasted little time when it came to getting Hendrix and *Hey Joe* together. Once the complete lineup of The Jimi Hendrix Experience was in place and a deal was struck to release a first single through Polydor/Track Records, the band repaired to De Lane Lea Studios, made famous as the place where Chandler's former band, The Animals, recorded their first hit single, *House of The Rising Sun*. They were there to record the first Jimi Hendrix Experience single, *Hey Joe,* for a rush release in the UK in December 1966.

Hendrix was not in the best shape, emotionally, as he prepared to enter the studio.

He was, doubtless, feeling just a touch homesick. He was overwhelmed at the lightning speed in which the business side of the recording industry seemed to function. A lot of rumor and speculation would ultimately arise about Hendrix's seeming insecurity and immaturity in the face of certain stardom. One story had it that the young musician, at one point, threw up his hands and told Chandler he was getting on a plane and going back to The States, thus ending his career before it started, and Chandler reportedly had to do his best talking to keep his explosive young charge in London. Another, more outlandish rumor had it that Chandler, not willing to lose money on the session, had a plan B backup, allegedly another band or singer, waiting in the proverbial wings that would take over the session if Hendrix bolted. Fortunately for all concerned, Hendrix came to his senses.

What was certain was that *Hey Joe* would be recorded on an extremely small studio budget, and that even the slightest slip up could be catastrophic. Kathy Etchingham, Hendrix's long-time girlfriend who met shortly after arriving in London, recalled in a *Daily Express* interview how a misstep during the *Hey Joe* session brought the wrath of Chandler down on her. "It was all done very quickly, because the studio was costing money. At one point, Chas shouted at me for opening the studio door when the red light was on because it blew the sound, and they had to do it again."

As acknowledged in the book *The Ultimate Hendrix: An Illustrated Encyclopedia of Live Concerts and Sessions*, those first hours recording *Hey Joe* were not boring. Hendrix, at that point, was still a babe in the woods when it came to the recording process, and it showed when the guitarist, unexpectedly, threw a tantrum when the session producer asked him to turn down the volume. There was also a lot of hand holding as Hendrix, nervously, contemplated singing on record for the first time. Those growing pains eventually subsided, as Hendrix set about recording what was, initially, going to be just one song: *Hey Joe*.

From the outset, it was agreed upon that *Hey Joe* would be the ideal way to introduce Jimi Hendrix to the world. But once in the studio there would be a difference of opinion as to what should be the B-side. In the *Hendrix Guide.com*, a detailed website of all things Hendrix, it was revealed that Hendrix wanted to do a cover of *Land of a Thousand Dances* as the flipside of *Hey Joe*, but Chandler insisted that Hendrix would be better served if he wrote an original song. The guitarist agreed, and went off to his creative corner to emerge sometime later with *Stone Free*.

In the studio, *Hey Joe* seemed to fit Hendrix like the proverbial glove, with truly powerful guitar arrangements full of fire, fury, volume and feedback, driving Hendrix's lost and lonely vocals. It also ultimately proved the ideal vehicle for the emergence of Hendrix from rock star to rock stud.

Author Hopkins, who delved long and hard into everything Hendrix for his book *The Jimi Hendrix Experience*, was all too familiar with the impact that The Experience's version of *Hey Joe* had had on the world as well as on himself. "There's no question that, from the opening chords of Jimi's guitar, that the song would become his for all time," he told the author. "Jimi, in a very public way, was the ultimate gunslinger. When the song opens with the question, 'Hey Joe, where you going with that gun in your hand?', you know, as the lyric plays out, that Jimi is not the interrogator, but, rather, he is Joe."

The recording studio was a new experience for Hendrix. This was made quite obvious during an early demo version of *Hey Joe*, as related in a *Songfacts.com,* when the guitarist was caught, unexpectedly, off guard, by the sound of his own voice in the headphones. Those privy to that primitive recording can clearly hear Hendrix saying "Oh Goddamn!" before turning to Chandler in the recording booth and saying, "Hey, make the voice a little lower, and the band a little louder."

The sound quality of the studio would turn out to be a bone of contention all through the recording of *Hey Joe*, with Chandler constantly complaining that the sound was not as good as it should be. For his part, The Leaves' Jim Pons would acknowledge in *Garagebands.com* that, initially, *Hey Joe* was a mixed bag. "I wasn't, initially knocked out by it. I really didn't think much about it at first. But I did consider it a compliment that Noel Redding used my bass line."

Hendrix would display a sense of unease during the *Hey Joe* recording session. "It was the first time I'd ever sung on record," he was quoted as saying in the Obrecht article. The time-sensitive nature of the *Hey Joe* session and the relative newness of the group dynamic would result in more than 30 takes being required to complete the song's backing tracks.

Hey Joe was released in the UK in December 1966, reportedly with songwriting credit on the single going to The Jimi Hendrix Experience, which would be quickly changed to Billy Roberts on subsequent pressings and the US release when the copyright hounds came around. It entered the UK Singles Chart in January 1967, and would spend approximately eight weeks on the charts before peaking at Number Six, according to *The Complete Book of British Charts*. According to *Billboard*, *Hey Joe* was released in the US in May 1967, but would fail to chart. But that didn't hurt The Experience's chances to crash America. The hype surrounding *Hey Joe* and Hendrix's extreme presentation had almost instantly paved the way for The Jimi Hendrix Experience to come to America.

Despite the fact that *Hey Joe* had a mediocre showing on the American charts, the buzz surrounding this wild-haired ex-pat and the equally wild song *Hey Joe* was definitely making people in the US music industry sit up and take notice. It also did not hurt when many superstar musicians from the UK were constantly singing Hendrix's praises. Especially when, at one point, the biggest outdoor rock festival in the United States was being organized. According to Genius.com, Paul McCartney and members of The Who were upfront in planting the Hendrix bug in the promoter's ears.

Their first live US appearance was nothing less than majestic. The band blasted *Hey Joe* out to literally thousands at the now-legendary Monterey Pop Festival. Always playful with the song in a live setting, during early concert appearances Hendrix would occasionally veer off the song's blueprint into an

Marc Shapiro

improvisational jag that included The Beatles' song *I Feel Fine*. And Hendrix was not above giving credit where credit was due. During a show in the East Village, Hendrix dedicated *Hey Joe* to Tim Rose. It was a sign of respect. It's too bad Rose could not have been equally complimentary, because when questioned about his feelings on Hendrix's version of what Rose continued to trumpet as his own personal creation, he said he absolutely hated it.

Chapter Five

The Floodgates Open

The success of The Jimi Hendrix Experiences' version of *Hey Joe* was both immediate and influential. It was the first version since The Leaves to hit the commercial charts, albeit the UK listings only, but it was suddenly the 'cool' song on a massive level, and a sign that *Hey Joe* had found its ride out of the underground and into the light of day.

Hendrix's *Hey Joe* sent millions of aspiring musicians racing into music stores to pick up the electric guitar. Using Hendrix's version as a jumping off point, it was possible during 1966-68 to go into any club, bar or concert hall and hear somebody out there tangling with *Hey Joe*. The song was everywhere. And it was the nature of the original song's construction that made it possible for musicians of various notoriety and ilk to attempt to put their own spin on the song.

Nineteen sixty-six saw The Cryan Shames and The Shadows of Knight, two bands that had a handful of minor regional, Midwest hits, include the song *Hey Joe* on their albums *Sugar & Spice* and *Back Door Men,* which would make some hay on *Hey Joe.* Even more obscure entries came from critics' favorites The Stillroven and The Ant Trip Ceremony who included *Hey Joe* on the only albums they recorded. *Hey Joe* also seemed to travel well internationally during this period. Noted French singer Johnny Hallyday included it on his *Olympia 67 album, singing it* with French lyrics, and Los Locos del Ritmo, recorded *Hey Joe* with Spanish lyrics on vinyl. Both artists performed the song in live performances.

In the case of Hallyday, a veteran French pop star whose bread and butter for many years had been taking popular international songs and doing French language versions of them, *Hey Joe* seemed a natural. Hallyday had allegedly had some live encounters with Hendrix well before he decided to record a French version of *Hey Joe*.

In late 1966, Hallyday's manager reportedly contacted Hendrix and his manager, Chas Chandler, and asked if Hendrix would like to be a part of Hallyday's backing band on an upcoming tour. Chandler said no, but said he would be interested in having The Jimi Hendrix Experience open for Hallyday for a short series of concerts. The result was that the French singer was up close and personal as Hendrix played *Hey Joe,* and proceeded to do a French cover not long after the conclusion of The Experience's portion of the tour.

That series of shows opening for Hallyday would be a rough and tumble coming out for The Jimi Hendrix Experience in general and *Hey Joe* in particular, according to the book *The Words and Music of Jimi Hendrix*. Slotted into a very short opening slot, the band literally only had time for four songs.

Consequently, Hendrix, who had early on made his bones on extended jams and lots of improvisation, was forced to cut back the set to the bare necessities. Of course, *Hey Joe* was the song those curious enough or hip enough to know all about Hendrix were there to see and hear. The feedback from those early reviews was mixed. With most of the crowd there to see Hallyday, the reaction to the opening act's over-the-top bombast was a mixture of amazement and sonic overload. Both were much in evidence during the band's truncated show. *Hey Joe* on record only hinted at the power and electric passion that the song brought in a live setting. It was a tough time for the band. They were still coming to grips with the vague nature of the music business, and the fact that while everybody around them were predicting superstardom, they were still dirt poor. But these first shots of *Hey Joe* rocketing through the Hallyday shows were a far from subtle hint of what was to come.

Back in The States, *Hey Joe* was, likewise, catching fire with the masses. It was even reported that a Midwest group called The Warlocks, (not The Warlocks who would later morph into The Grateful Dead, who were also known to play *Hey Joe* on occasion) had managed to put out an album that contained their version of *Hey Joe*.

Around the time of the Warlocks' version of *Hey Joe*, another unknown act was cutting its earliest recording teeth on the song. The Buoys recorded a fairly straightforward pop rock rendition of *Hey Joe* on the regional Pamela label. The record did bupkis, but The Buoys would push on and eventually found pop culture fame—or perhaps infamy—when they teamed up with future big shot songwriter Rupert Holmes to rack up a Top 20 chart single about cannibalism called *Timothy*.

Devil's Own out of Portsmouth, New Hampshire, was typical of countless regional bands whose lone brush with 'stardom' centered around *Hey Joe*. Devil's Own were big on the Portsmouth teen club circuit from 1966 to 68, before going the way of all garage-band flesh, but *Hey Joe* would be their masterstroke. Recorded as the A-side of a single on Exit Records (the B-side being Willie Dixon's *I Just Wanna Make Love*), the single hit the charts on November 28, 1966 on Portsmouth's WBBX. The single, an okay version of *Hey Joe* done up very Leaves style, would plateau at Number 16 on the local charts, ahead of such acts as The Righteous Brothers, Jr. Walker and The All Stars, The Temptations and Herman's Hermits.

Nineteen sixty-seven was turning out to be the year when all-things-music were possible. The sheer simplicity of *Hey Joe* was proving a driving force in thousands of young teen garage bands, learning the basic chord structure necessary for their perfect *Hey Joe*. An East Coast teen club band called The Castiles was one of those who took their covers of *Hey Joe* and other songs that they could learn from the Top 40 stations, and became darlings of the burgeoning "18 and under" teen shows, before going off and having less cool lives. So why do The Castiles merit this much space? Two reasons: they left behind a recording called *Live at The Left Foot Teen Club, St. Peters Church, Freehold, New Jersey, Jan 1967*, and there was this little matter of the band's guitarist and lead singer. He was a kid named Bruce Springsteen. Years later, in an interview with *The Guardian,* he said that his face would light up when he heard the old Castiles' tapes. What brought the smile to Springsteen's face was the way the Castiles tried to sound hip, punctuating *Hey Joe* with a requisite number of "uhs, ooo's, 'alrights' and 'dig its' amidst their slightly psychedelic rendition.

But of all the countless garage bands across the US, a Grand Rapids, Michigan band dubbed The Soul Benders easily deserves an honorable mention as a band that got a lot out of *Hey Joe,* though it ultimately went nowhere.

On the surface, The Soul Benders were the prototypical garage band of the day: lots of enthusiasm, but varying degrees of talent. What seemingly set them apart was the bit of daring the band took on the strength of songs like *Love's 7 &7 Is.* Then they made their first attempt at recording *Hey Joe.*

In a conversation with *60'sGaragebands.com,* former Soul Bender's keyboardist and front man Aris Hampers remembered what happened when a miniscule 1000 record pressing of *Hey Joe* hit the streets of Grand Rapids. It magically went to Number One on all three of Grand Rapid's top rock radio stations.

"The first run of 1000 copies sold out in two days," he related. "I was stunned. I did another order of 1000 copies and those were gone by the end of the second week. I ordered one more run of 1000 copies while our version of *Hey Joe* was still Number One on the charts and pretty quickly they were all gone by the time the song was just starting to fall down the charts. It was still pretty high up there when we ran out of records, but I decided not to push my luck and did not order more."

The regional success of *Hey Joe* put The Soul Benders within spitting distance of a major label deal, Hampers recalled. "*Hey Joe* would spend six weeks at Number One in Grand Rapids, and word was getting out to some of the major labels that it was a top seller. At one point, I got a phone call from somebody at Atco Records who wanted more information on the record and the band. At the time, Atco didn't have much going on rock-wise with the exception of Cream, and were pretty much a straight ahead pop and rhythm and blues label. So, I just said something stupid like, 'I'd like a better label to put out our record.' "

It was not long after Hampers said "Thanks, but no thanks" to Atco that the label went on a rock signing spree, landing such budding superstars as The Iron Butterfly, Vanilla Fudge and The Allman Brothers. As for The Soul Benders, it was a quick demise into the annals of obscurity, according to Hampers. "I sometimes wonder if things might have been different if I had just kept my mouth shut."

For better or worse, one of the first to tackle *Hey Joe* in an extremely blatant, very uncool and commercial way was as far away from the Hendrix sphere of influence as one could conceivably get. It was Cher. Cher always seemed to have that tough girl, street savvy persona lurking somewhere in her musical psyche, but even keen observers rarely saw beyond the glitz and pop sparkle. By the time she recorded her album *With Love, Cher,* it seemed as if she had totally succumbed to the commercially viable and catchy pop vibe, safer than daring.

That was why more than one critic raised an eyebrow when Cher chose to include *Hey Joe* (as well as Bob Dylan's *The Times They Are a Changing*) in amongst the album's fluff and pap. But give credit where credit is due: the singer gave *Hey Joe* her best shot. She was comfortable with the subject matter, and given her glossy, uptown reputation, she sounded fairly tough and real amidst the lightweight hippie chic/psychedelia of her then-husband and partner in crime Sonny Bono.

What to many seemed even more daring was that Cher and her record company, in a not too veiled attempt at breaking with her image, chose to release *Hey Joe* as a single. Critics were quick to pounce on her effort, proclaiming that her *Hey Joe* was uneven and ultimately too far afield from her previous musical output to be considered anything but a gimmick. But Cher's version of *Hey Joe* would chart in the US, coming in at a very modest Number 94 on the Top 100 before sinking into oblivion.

Hey Joe would be better served when Wilson Pickett wrapped his more compatible musical hands around it. Pickett had made his rhythm and blues bones by alternating originals and revved up covers, done in his alternately screaming and soul tones. And it was with covers and commercial hits in mind that Pickett entered Fame Studios in 1968 with the Muscle Shoals Rhythm Section, a legendary session ensemble known for their ability to play any style at any time, to knock out a trio of potential hits. The slam dunk of the bunch would be The Beatles' *Hey Jude*, followed by a sure bet for the rhythm and blues market, *Mini Skirt Minnie*. It would be almost as an afterthought for Pickett to try his hand at *Hey Joe*.

Maxwell Pickett, the late singer's brother,

personal assistant and currently the CEO of the highly informative *Wilsonpickett.com*, told this author that, "The cover of *Hey Joe* was greatly influenced by the success of *Hey Jude* by The Beatles. That song was successful, and we believed that following up *Hey Jude* with *Hey Joe* gave the song a running start on the charts. The song was not a hard sell. Radio stations played it a lot."

In Pickett's hands *Hey Joe* would turn out to be a crackling, whip smart screamer that critics would praise as a raw, back alley addition to the *Hey Joe* dossier, with soulful moving vocals and its own sense of wild-eyed danger. As it would turn out, this version of *Hey Joe* would surprise many in its across-the-board appeal. The song would hit Number 29 on the US Rhythm & Blues charts, climb to Number 59 on the US Pop charts, climb to Number 42 on the Canadian bestseller list, and finally hit Number 16 on the UK charts. Pickett's brother was not surprised at the song's success.

"He really loved to sing that song," he recalled. "Wilson brought to *Hey Joe* what he brought to every song he recorded, which was that raw southern soul. Wilson had a sound all of his own, and he was hot at the time. Everything he touched turned out well, and *Hey Joe* was a perfect example."

Overlooked in the rush to get *Hey Joe* on vinyl was the nifty little bit of lyric hoodoo perpetrated by singer Johnny Rivers on his 1968 album *Realization*. Rivers noted in a passage in the book *60's Rock: Garage, Psychedelic and Other Satisfactions*, that in a moment of whacked out creative license, he decided to not only rewrite nearly all of the lyrics in the song, but also to change the traditional question and answer conceit into just that Joe's friend asks the questions and Joe does not respond.

Rivers' lyric sleight of hand may well have been the last hurrah in terms of monkeying with the original lyrical structure of *Hey Joe* in hopes of snagging the writing credit. Because, at that point, no matter what kind of tinkering was being done, the bottom line was that Billy Roberts was credited as the hands down author of *Hey Joe*.

By the mid-60's, it appeared that the whole question of authorship of *Hey Joe* had slowly but surely resolved itself. Hillel Resner had, by this time, taken over as Billy Roberts' manager, and his main duties seemed to be keeping track of *Hey Joe*. "I was handling all his publishing affairs and collecting his royalties on *Hey Joe*," he related to *Hey Joe Versions*. "With the numerous covers of *Hey Joe* having come out, not to mention the seemingly unending Jimi Hendrix versions, those royalties were substantial."

But "substantial royalties" from *Hey Joe* did not necessarily translate into Roberts living high on the hog. In fact, the opposite was largely true. Roberts, in actions and deeds, seemed very much committed to the folksinger/bohemian lifestyle despite the success of *Hey Joe*, spending freely and easily, preferring the itinerant rather than opulent lifestyle.

In a memoir that appeared in *Hey Joe Versions*, musician Bill Stapleton, a contemporary of Roberts, recalled that, by 1972, "The *Hey Joe* song royalties didn't seem to keep him [Roberts] totally afloat." Stapleton further recalled that on one occasion Roberts and a group of fellow musicians set up shop in front of a Bank of America building to earn enough money to get a few drinks and something to eat.

What Roberts did with the royalty money was not a huge concern to Resner. But tracking down royalties was, and, as he would regularly find out, it was not always an easy task. Despite the fact that ownership of *Hey Joe* had been legally changed to Billy Roberts, there would occasionally be a situation where a *Hey Joe* cover was still being attributed to Dino Valenti. That had to be straightened out. Exhibit A: N. Jama Santers, who claimed in a comment to *Hey Joe Versions* that she had been Valenti's' 'old lady' between 1976 and 1983 and during those seven years, said that "He [Dino] received quarterly royalty statements from BMI (the song publishing organization), and they included in the numerous song credits and royalties...the song *Hey Joe*." Adding more fuel to the controversy was the lingering impression in many quarters that *Hey Joe* was a traditional song, and as such was open to having anybody who recorded the song automatically entitled to authorship credit.

One of the first to take advantage of this legal dance around Roberts' duly noted and registered title as author of *Hey Joe* was the progressive heavy metal band Deep Purple. The British band was formed on a wing and a prayer. They gathered a handful of originals and covers and were rushed into the studio, given three days to record an entire album. That would ultimately be entitled *Shades of Deep Purple*. From the start, Deep Purple were centered on a more experimental and far reaching metal style, which, when it came to doing a nearly eight minute *Hey Joe*, meant throwing everything and the kitchen sink into the mix.

Purple's version of *Hey Joe* was a literal mélange of classical influences (snippets of *The Miller's Dance, Suite No.2 Part 2 of El Sombrero des tres picos ballet* by Manuel de Falla and a racing rhythm reminiscent of Ravel's *Bolero*) in an extended intro, and final guitar/keyboard flame up. The vocals held center stage in the middle third of the song, and this was the only familiar element, for anybody looking for the classic *Hey Joe* elements.

The band was so full of themselves that they decided their version of *Hey Joe* was their unique creation, and thus credited themselves as the songwriters. By the time Deep Purple signed a record deal and *Shades of Deep Purple* was released, word had gotten back to Resner, and Deep Purple received the obligatory cease and desist order. Roberts' name was quickly inserted as author. Deep Purple would ultimately receive their just rewards. They were the creators of the most bombastic and theatrical version of *Hey Joe* most likely ever put to vinyl.

From the mid-60's on, the Scottish pop/rock band Marmalade was one of the top hit makers on both sides of the Atlantic. That popularity meant the band was always in a mad race to get out new material. Such was the case in 1968 when they were about to release their new single *Lovin' Things.* The only problem was that the band did not have a B-side to the single, and the clock was ticking. That's when *Hey Joe* entered the picture.

Marmalade felt they were on safe ground with *Hey Joe* because, like many others, they felt the song was traditional material and thus up for grabs to anybody who wanted to take songwriting credit. To their credit, Marmalade did a crackling good rendition, very much in the realm of Hendrix's. It served as a harder counter to the A-side, and would later turn up as track ten on Marmalade's album *There's a Lot of It About*.

The band was in clover. Marmalade guitarist Junior Campbell described it in the *I See The Rain: The CBS Years' 2003 CD Liner Notes*, "The Jimi Hendrix version of *Hey Joe* had already sold around 200,000 copies, and then we sold around 300,000 copies of the flip of *Lovin' Things*. But then about a year later the bloke who'd written the bloody song turned up out of the woodwork." Marmalade joined the select group of performers who had gotten caught with their hand in the *Hey Joe* cookie jar and were legally induced to make the appropriate songwriting credit change to Billy Roberts.

The impact of Hendrix's fiery version of *Hey Joe* served as a guidepost to many of the bands attempting their interpretation of the song. Lots of loud guitar and loud just about everything else seemed the way to go. Owing to the nature of the music business and the often-unpredictable nature of musicians, many of the superior covers of the song are hard to find.

One that has escaped the attention of many was The Guess Who's take on *Hey Joe* which, for posterity, has been relegated to a bootleg entitled *Live In Winnepeg 1967*. The Guess Who, whose radio friendly brand of pop/rock made them commercial darlings for the better part of a decade, took the occasion of this live setting to tear into the song, borrowing unabashedly from the Hendrix version, and turning in a surprisingly intense outing.

Nineteen sixty-seven would also be the year that a fairly unknown Midwest band called The James Gang were blasting out a fairly heavy version of *Hey Joe* at places like The Chesterland Hullabaloo in Ohio, before their hits *'Walk Away'* and *'Funk #49* (along with the addition of guitarist Joe Walsh), put the band on the national map.

Switzerland was light years removed from Ohio but even in the land of peace, progressive thinking and more blondes than you could shake a stick at, the influence of *Hey Joe* was evident when a band of enterprising locals called The Attacks pooled their money together and pressed 100 copies of their debut disc, entitled *We Call It Attackology*, which featured *Hey Joe* sung in their native tongue. If you happen to be lucky enough to have a copy of *We Call It Attackology*, consider yourself truly blessed.

The onset of teen dance clubs and battle of the bands shows continued to draw crowds, especially in places that rarely saw sunshine or an A list band. Enthusiasm at these events usually overrode explosive talent and *Hey Joe*, courtesy of bands and audiences that lived and died by the local top 40 radio stations, was, more often than not, a welcome guest. One band that was typical of the times was Zero End. The Pacific Northwest band managed to snag enough local stardom to land a label deal with Garland Records and, in 1966, released *Hey Joe* as the A-side of the first of two singles.

Around the same time Zero End was tearing things up in the Pacific Northwest, Detroit was unleashing its own measure of *Hey Joedom* with the group The Del Tinos, whose 1966 album *The Del*

*Tinos Meet The Hesitations: Go, Go, Go To Surfin'
School* on the notorious Norton Records label, featured
a rocking version of *Hey Joe*. The band managed to
parlay *Hey Joe* and a whole lot of 60's rock covers
into a three-year gig in and around the Motor City
before packing up their instruments and going home.
What sounds like another short-lived stint on the road
to real life was made worthy of notice when The Del
Tino's guitar player, a cat named Cub Koda would,
some years later, find a niche in rock and roll annals in
the band Brownsville Station and the song *Smokin'In
The Boys Room*.

Hey Joe would come to play an important role in
the musical development of Rudi Protrudi (The
Fuzztones) when, as a member of the Pennsylvania
band King Arthur's Quart. The band was just another
teen combo on the hunt back in 1966 when they
recorded *King Arthur's Quart: Live at Allen Jr. High
School*. The recording was, admittedly, rank amateur
but, in the case of *Hey Joe*, the very low fi nature of
the recording made their version kind of cute in a
pimply kid angst sort of way. The recording made the
informal neighborhood rounds and then disappeared
along with the band. Strangely enough, 700 copies
would emerge in the mid 90's via Misty Lane Records.
On the liner notes of the recording, Protrudi laughingly
acknowledged, "Who would have thought people
might be interested in hearing recordings of my very
first band? We were about as amateur as you could
get."

Remember The Ultimate Spinach? Cool,
psychedelic/acid/freakout music. Cool name. Let's
face it, you'd better be good if you're going to call

yourselves The Ultimate Spinach. Don't worry, there is a *Hey Joe* angle to all this. Shortly after the band formed in Boston in 1966, they released 50 copies of a promotional, not for sale disc *The Ultimate Spinach at The Coffee House Lounge*. *Hey Joe* was on the disc and it was groovy, slightly surreal and threatening, in the best possible way. This bit of vinyl is as rare as…well you get the picture. Long story short, promo leads to a big label deal with MGM, the band does two good albums, *The Ultimate Spinach* and *Behold and See*, before calling it quits. One bit of trivia surrounding The Spinach. A second album guitar replacement was a very young Jeff 'Skunk' Baxter who would go on to fame and fortune as a member of both Steely Dan and The Doobie Brothers. Neither of which have ever recorded versions of *Hey Joe*. Too bad because that would be way cool.

Meanwhile back out west, the horn heavy Chicago Transit Authority (who would later rechristen themselves Chicago and add hits and stardom to their resume) were just getting their act together which meant playing a lot of sets at a lot of clubs which, in turn, necessitated a whole lot of covers. Although CTA already had more than enough originals for what would be their daring debut two record set, there is some evidence to indicate that they could be fiery when playing other people's material. Most notably was a thundering take on *Hey Joe* that would regularly be trotted out during the band's salad days. In their hands, it was rocking and bluesy, aided and abetted by screaming guitar licks and an early bank of horns. While *Hey Joe* did not make the cut on their first album (an equally powerful *I'm A Man* did), *Hey Joe* would make it onto a 1968 bootleg entitled *Chicago Transit Authority: Live at Barnaby Chicago June 1968*.

But *Hey Joe* was not all serious business in the mid-60s. A lot of bands, with tongue firmly planted in cheek, wanted to have fun with the song. They got really out there. As chronicled by author Michael Hicks in his book *Sixties Rock: Garage, Psychedelic and Other Satisfactions*, such was the case with Group Therapy who, in 1968, conceived the first gay version of *Hey Joe*. In that take, the song was typically rave up rock and roll until the very end, when each stanza of the phrase 'Hey Joe' was followed by the singer pleading 'I need you!', 'Don't leave me,' and finally, 'I love you.' Pretty hair curling stuff for the time, but a version that would ultimately pale in infamy to the *Hey Joe* cover entitled *To Masturbate* by the group Mad Sound. Essentially a straight up cover punctuated by vocals primarily consisting of, and let's be delicate here, the very obvious sounds of self- gratification. Finally, with a nod to feet fetishism and torture, the mid-60s group The Hazards gave their double barrel blast of *Hey Joe* a slice of real menace when they intoned that Joe was going to do something unintelligible to his woman's feet because she had been running around on him.

Round about 1968 a Birmingham England band called Band of Joy was scuffling around the local UK scene, trying to get noticed. The band was notable for having future members of Led Zeppelin, Robert Plant and John Bonham in their lineup. Slightly less notable was the fact that one of their roadies was Noddy Holder, who would go on to his own degree of celebrity as a member of the band Slade. The band, apparently in the midst of management squabbles, went into the studio and recorded some demos in an attempt to woo a recording contract. Among the songs included in the demo tapes was a truly riveting version of *Hey Joe*. How anybody could refuse cutting a deal with a band that featured Plant and Bonham is now unthinkable. But when Band of Joy could not interest a label the band broke up, although lineup changes would keep the band semi-active for another year or so. *Hey Joe* would linger in Plant's consciousness. In 2003 a Robert Plant retrospective album, *Sixty Six to Timbuktu*, would contain Plant's old Band of Joy version of *Hey Joe*.

From the beginning, *Hey Joe*, in lyrical content and tone, seemed ripe for parody, and, to a degree, cynicism and outrage. In the hands of Frank Zappa & The Mothers of Invention, it was a perfect fit.

For the album *'We're Only In It For The Money'* (1968), Zappa seemed in a particularly derisive and cynical mood, which resulted in several songs on the album poking massive holes in several pop culture untouchables of the day. As it turned out, Zappa had a particular bone to pick with the suddenly fashionable and blatant commercial exploitation of the hippie lifestyle, hence the tongue in cheek putdown of *Flower Punk,* which included a generous dose of *Hey Joe,* adding some clever new lyrics. To wit: "Hey Punk, where you going with that flower in your hand?/ Well I'm going up to Frisco to join a psychedelic band."

Musically, *Flower Punk* was pure Zappa: just enough of an homage to know where the source material came from. Then, according to what longtime

Mothers of Invention band member Don Preston said in an interview with the author in 2015, "Basically what Zappa did was that he took the chord changes from the original *Hey Joe* [or as most refer to it today, the Hendrix version]. "Then he turned the music into a bunch of 5/8th and 7/8th notes. He used the same rhythmic structure of the melody but he used different notes."

Preston, who was in the band when *Flower Punk* was recorded late in 1967 and is now a spirited 82 year-old, admitted to his memory being a bit light on certain aspects of Zappa's *Hey Joe*, and then turned to a nearby keyboard and knocked out an impromptu version of *Hey Joe* to refresh his memory. He conceded that, like most of Zappa's songs, this send up of *Hey Joe* was largely a Zappa creation.

"Zappa did all the vocals and all the three part harmonies," recalled Preston. "It was basically Frank's version of the song done Frank's way. The band didn't have much influence on the song. We would add certain notes along the way. Frank sang all the melodies and the comedy parts. Basically, we would add things. It was a lot of 4/5th and 4/7th notes. Frank sang all the melodies and the comedy parts. On that song, the band would add things that Frank knew we already knew. The basic tracks probably took a couple of hours. Then Frank would spend weeks doing other things to it."

Preston recalled that Frank Zappa and The Mothers of Invention would play *Flower Punk* live on a fairly regular basis. And even by Zappa's demanding standards, the result was worth the effort. "I thought the finished song was very good," said Preston. "It had a very fast tempo which was the kind of thing that was pretty much unheard of in rock and roll at the time."

The late-60's would see what many considered the first super group of the modern era, Blind Faith. With the likes of Eric Clapton and Steve Winwood leading the charge, and with no shortage of collective egos in the group, it would only be a matter of time before Blind Faith would combust. Not surprisingly the band broke up after only one album and one tour. But those with their mind on the bottom line made sure that everything connected with Blind Faith was recorded, both for posterity and for profit. When the band entered a rehearsal studio in 1969 the entire session was put down on tape. As it would turn out, the first take of an instrumental jam centered around *Hey Joe*, and clocking in at a shade under six minutes it would ultimately be released in Italy years after the band called it quits, under the title *Blind Faith: Rehearsals.*

By the end of the decade, *Hey Joe* was everywhere in the repertoire of both obscure and A-list acts. In fact, it was hard to find a band that did not play *Hey Joe*. The song appeared in quite a number of live bootlegs, a number of European and Asian-only EP's and albums, and, to the consternation of avid collectors, unreleased snippets.

The Allman Brothers' live performance of *Hey Joe*, entitled, simply, *Allman Brothers Hey Joe March 30, 1969*, was a mammoth ten-plus-minute workout of the song, featuring fiery guitar work by the late Duane Allman and recorded at the Jacksonville Armory in Florida. It remains a must-hear and a must-have for band and song fanatics alike. Another mythical outing, also unreleased and rarely heard, is Booker T & The MG's hot and sweaty version of *Hey Joe* from a June 8, 1968 live performance at Winterland in San Francisco. Even the very good but equally short-lived blues supergroup The Electric Flag managed to squeeze out as many as four live performances containing various length versions of *Hey Joe*. They were released in Europe on *The Electric Flag at The Carousel Ballroom* (on an English CBS label) and *Electric Flag: Gravenites and Bloomfield.*

Going into the tail end of the 60's, *Hey Joe* had become the go-to song. For many, the song was an easily accessed album cut. Groups had hopes of turning the song into yet another commercial hit a la Hendrix.

And then there was Fever Tree, who, to a very large extent, were pinning their hopes on *Hey Joe* to keep their career going

Chapter Six

Joe's Got The Fever

Fever Tree, out of Houston, Texas, seemed destined for little more than regional success. The band had a fairly good handle on psychedelia, and maintained enough drama from their pre-rock, folk group days to manage to pay the bills. But Fever Tree got lucky right from the start. The idea of writing their own songs and reaping the financial benefits had not reached Houston yet, and so Fever Tree was content to gobble up everything offered up by their producers and respected songwriters Scott and Vivian Holtzman. The result was that Fever Tree was the recipient of a slice of commercial pop/psychedelia called *San Francisco Girls (Return of The Native)* that was a passable West Coast hit that managed to snag a lower end of the Top 100 Billboard chart in 1968.

Fever Tree's keyboard player Rob Landes looked back on those days in a 2015 interview with this author and recalled that, in the wake of *San Francisco Girls (Return of The Native)* things were looking good for the band. "We were touring a lot. We were doing a lot of press, and we had billboards up in Los Angeles. At that point we were riding high."

Their first album, titled *Fever Tree*, made enough chart noise to get the band within knocking distance of the big time. But when a second album, *Another Time, Another Place,* and a third, *Creation*, did not produce the much-needed smash hit, Fever Tree, amid internal squabbles, substance issues and the frustration of being so close but not close enough, was nearing the end of its run. That's when *Hey Joe* entered the picture.

Fever Tree was contractually obligated to do one more album, and the band just didn't have their hearts in it. Landes was still in the band in name only, and he recalled that the group was about to cut ties with the Holtzmans, who, in a last minute attempt to resurrect their fortunes, brought in a number of outtakes and older band material and a handful of covers designed to patch together a reasonable album. Among the songs suggested was *Hey Joe*.

"We thought *Hey Joe* would be a good song to do," recalled Landes. "It had that sense of rawness that we felt we could do. And those of us who were still talking to each other felt we could do something in terms of doing something psychedelic with it. At that point, we were fed up with each other and the band, and agreed to do *Hey Joe* just to get it all over with."

Fever Tree had to be dragged into the studio to record *Hey Joe* as part of a half- hearted album that would be titled *For Sale.* As the fates would have it, their version of *Hey Joe* would become something of an underground/cult item. The initial attitude had been to go into the studio and knock out a perfunctory three or four-minute cover, and call it a day. But amid the band's collective lousy attitude, a creative spark was lit, and the result was a highly evocative mixture of long (naysayers say too long), instrumental psychedelic passages, coupled with an overall sense of tragedy rather than the notion of revenge that had permeated most *Hey Joe* covers. It was far from perfect, but, in a psychologically raw and damaged way, it definitely had its moments.

Ever the optimist, Landes had to admit to this author that "the result is the worst hodgepodge of sound you've ever heard in your life. But all things being equal, I guess you'd have to say that our version of *Hey Joe* sounded pretty good."

Released in 1970, *For Sale* landed, not surprisingly, with a thud. Nothing on the album was worthy of radio consideration. But even the most savage reviews had to admit that Fever Tree's version of *Hey Joe*, warts and all, was the diamond in this "nothing" record. Over the next 20 years, Fever Tree would break up, reform and break up again. It existed primarily for touring purposes, and to turn a buck. Consequently, there remain a scattering of live videos of the band performing *Hey Joe.*

Not everything involving *Hey Joe* was predictable and planned out. There were those spontaneous moments in which the song was a phantom, making an appearance as part of an unexpected and joyous bit of noise. Such was the case on September 4, 1970 when the band Led Zeppelin, freshly anointed as the next big thing, had just completed a headlining performance at the famed Los Angeles Forum, when they decided to crash somebody else's party. In this case it was at the legendary—but much more sedate—confines of The Troubadour, where that night British folk-rockers Fairport Convention were holding court to a much smaller audience than Zeppelin's had been.

Who was more surprised, the band or the audience? That was open to conjecture. But when the members of Led Zeppelin showed up on The Troubadour stage, one thing was certain. The party was on. And so over a jam session that lasted more than three hours, the combined bands played anything and everything, including what was reportedly a fiery version of *Hey Joe*.

The 70's saw a flood of pretenders to the *Hey Joe* throne. It seemed like everybody had caught the fever and was attempting to work the song out in any number of ways. One of the more interesting attempts came at the hands of soul singer and guitarist Lee Moses, who delivered in a very deep, grinding turn on *Hey Joe*, on his album *Time and Peace*. The album was a commercial failure, but his rendition of *Hey Joe* was first rate, thanks to the contributions of funk monsters The Ohio Players.

Largely known for their popularity in Europe were The Les Humphries Singers, a derivation of The Edwin Hawkins Singers who delivered pop and country-influenced covers with the fervor of gospel. It would be an attitude that made their version of *Hey Joe* somewhat of a head scratcher to the casual listener but, in its own way, was an arresting obscurity, appearing on their album *We'll Fly You To The Promised Land*.

Hey Joe was cause celebration for the Australian band Carson. Carson, an enticing mixture of country, blues and foot stomping boogie, were the Down Under version of America's Canned Heat, and *Hey Joe* could be the anthem for their party. They made a point of driving their roots home with a fist-pumping, live workout on their album *On The Air.*

In 1974, legendary blues and folk guitarist Roy Buchannan took a stab at *Hey Joe,* and the result was a haunting and subtly wrought version on his album *That's What I Am Here For.* For his part, Buchannan offered up a heartfelt dedication to Hendrix, who, by that time, was four years in the ground.

The call to *Hey Joe* had reached mammoth proportions by the start of the 70's. The song was being used as a template to jump into any number of established musical genres, as well as some that were just coming into their own.

There would be another artful dedication to Hendrix in the year that Buchannan put his down for posterity. It would easily turn out to be the most daring versions of *Hey Joe* to come along since…well… Jimi's.

Chapter Seven

Patti's Got a Gun

Going into 1970, Patti Smith was at the head of the class when it came to taking music to that next big step. More intellectual than calculating, Smith came from a literary place. She was a deep and philosophically dark poetess in execution, and artistic in her individual, creative scheme of things. Smith had made her name as a street style poet, melding pop and punk stylings and attitudes that had been embraced by the growing New York City underground. Smith's path and the world of rock and roll were destined to collide, and by 1970 she was exploring a brazen musical experience that, among other things, had no need of a drummer.

Patti Smith gave off the aura of tough street chick, but the reality was that she was introspective and extremely shy in the face of her growing notoriety. On the night of August 26, 1970, Smith, despite having a formal invite to a party celebrating the official opening of Electric Lady Studios and the driving force behind its creation, The Jimi Hendrix Experience, Smith was way too shy to mix and mingle for very long, and soon found herself spending much of the evening loitering outside on the steps of the studio. At one point, the star of the show, Jimi Hendrix, came outside and sat down beside her.

After a few tense moments of uneasy silence, Smith broke the ice.

"I said I was too shy to go in," she recalled in an interview with *The Observer*, "and he said 'I'm shy, and that's why I'm leaving.' We talked for a bit and he told me his plans. He told me he was off to catch a plane to England for the Isle of Wight Festival. But he would never come back."

Three weeks after speaking easily with Smith, Jimi Hendrix was dead. Smith would be distraught at the news, recalling on a daily basis the meeting with a true genius of a man, and imagining the great things he would have done if he had lived. She was heartbroken, but she would go on with her life.

By 1974 Smith had grown confident enough in her creative abilities to take that all-important first step of recording her music. It would be a modest effort: a two-sided seven-inch single. The B-side would be an original composition called *Piss Factory,* about the agony of getting through the day. If she stretched her meager budget, she was hoping to press 2000 copies. It would be recorded in Electric Lady Studios. To further pay homage to Hendrix, the A-side would be *Hey Joe*.

"Going into the Electric Lady Studio to record *Hey Joe*, I felt a real sense of duty," she told *The Observer*. "I was very conscious that I was getting to do something that he [Hendrix] didn't."

On June 5, 1974, Patti Smith's first-ever recorded words were "Hi, Jimi." But what followed made a whole different animal out of the preconceived notions of what *Hey Joe* was all about. Smith immediately launched into a fairly long introductory song-poem about Patti Hearst and her legendary abduction and crime spree with the notorious *Symbionese Liberation Army*. Alternately sly, salacious and emotionally jarring, the story/poem cuts to a new essence of what *Hey Joe* ultimately means, and what the potential was for the original song's meaning.

The arrangement of the song, proper, was also blazingly different, as befitting Smith's creative standards. She was an enticing rock body, moving in and out of the blues amalgam of Roy Buchannan's best licks and attitudes, spring boarding her into free flowing flights of plaintive vocals, and raw, animal emotion. The body of the record is, with a gender change or two, the classic *Hey Joe*. It whips through the intent of Hendrix, and in the best possible way takes the all-too-familiar song into new and unknown regions of thought before reintroducing Hearst and her tale of coming-of-age in a world suddenly full of raw emotion and survival, and miles away from the vacuum of privilege.

Hey Joe had suddenly and unexpectedly become a signpost up ahead for a new age. Once critics stopped falling all over themselves saying Hendrix's version was the definitive cover of *Hey Joe*, there would be few that would argue with the notion that Patti Smith's version was the next best cover ever.

This was a time when Disco, for better or worse, was the reigning form in popular music, but that did not stop a thriving underground of expressive and defiant musicians from digging in their heels and dragging *Hey Joe* back into the spotlight for another go round.

Led Zeppelin took the hint.

Based on their 1970 Troubadour appearance, the band had proven themselves more than capable of mixing it up. When The Hendrix Tribute, an All-Star Concert, was conceived in 1974, it made perfect sense that Led Zeppelin would be on board. It made even more sense that they would once again attach themselves to *Hey Joe*, this time in a less jam, and more straight-ahead concert atmosphere. It would be a rousing success. The band's pure heaviness coupled with Robert Plant's screaming, plaintive vocals struck at the heart of Hendrix's vision of the song, and, to this day, this is a version that purists look to as one of the best.

To this day, Spirit remains one of the most woefully underappreciated bands of the past 40 years. This progressive group is often mentioned in the same breath as Led Zeppelin, but by the mid-70's the band was in the midst of yet another lineup change, and were celebrating their latest record deal with a massive two-disc undertaking entitled *The Spirit of 76* (released in 1975). Spirit guitarist Randy California, who had played with and befriended Hendrix back in the day, had turned into a monster of a player in his own right, and so it seemed almost appropriate for the band to do a version of *Hey Joe*. Spirit's version would be very much in the tradition of Hendrix's, offering up guitar pyrotechniques and a savage, bluesy bottom.

That newly minted 70's super group Bad Company would cross paths with *Hey Joe* is not surprising. The band, rooted in raw rock and primitive, bottom-heavy blues made them a natural for the song, and it quickly became a pivotal moment in most of their late 70's live performances that, in many cases, reintroduced audiences to a song they may have been too young or too oblivious to know the first time around. Bad Company was at their peak on August 31, 1979 in a concert at The Capitol Center in Landover, Maryland. Over time, four different versions of that show have become hot items on the bootleg circuit, with *Hey Joe* driving the recording's success.

Hey Joe also succeeded in bringing a musician full circle who had shared the biggest concert event, Woodstock, with Hendrix.

Alvin Lee had taken a shining to *Hey Joe* in the late 70's. Already well past his prime as the leader of the legendary blues-rockers Ten Years After, Lee had been on a hiatus of sorts, issuing the occasional solo album and touring at his leisure. But sensing that his real cache was in people's memories of Ten Years After, Lee decided to go where the interest was. He formed a power trio called Ten Years Later, and their first album *Ride On* (1979) featured an all-so-bluesy workout of *Hey Joe*. Ten Years Later toured for a time, and it became evident to those who saw the band or had seen grainy concert videos, that Lee, in *Hey Joe*, had found a raw, racing, face-distorting substitute for his classic, *I'm Going Home*.

Chapter Eight

The 80'S Go Hey

Things were rough for a struggling young actor named Thomas Jane in the 1980's. At age 18, the man who would go on to have a solid career highlighted by a starring role in *The Punisher*, was literally homeless on the streets of Hollywood, living in a car and struggling to get enough to eat. He was down and out with no prospects. In his lowest moment, he turned to the song *Hey Joe* for help.

"I didn't have any money," he said in conversations with *Under The Radar* and *Monsters & Critics*, "so I bought a guitar and busked on the streets of Hollywood. I only knew two songs, and one of them was *Hey Joe*. People used to pelt me with change just to shut me up. But I managed to eat with that money for quite a while." It did not get any more dramatic for *Hey Joe* during the decade of the 80's than that. It was not that *Hey Joe* was sleeping, or that the song had lost its umph. The song was definitely in play, but the play, for the most part, was running below the radar.

On the up side, the decade of the 80's was easily one of the more diverse times for the song, as musicians with various degrees of notoriety and styles continued to embrace what had long-since become a standard in popular music.

One of the more tantalizing blips on the screen was 80's Los Angeles band Failsafe, a new wave, snarky and musically diverse ensemble, that were way out there, covering live, music from movies *In Like Flynt* and *The World of Suzie Wong*. Easily their most memorable slice of quirk was a neither fish nor fowl workout of *Hey Joe* that challenged at every turn, and was ambitious in its abandon. Failsafe produced two albums and an EP over a three-year span, but faded into obscurity.

Inevitably, *Hey Joe* was proving quite adaptable to just about any genre of music in the 80's, and was finding particular favor with the metal and progressive rock scenes in Europe. Exhibit A: the very obscure but nevertheless interesting More.

More was never more (no pun intended) than an also-ran in the European heavy metal surge of the 1980's. The band had the distinction of having in their midst the very first Iron Maiden singer, Paul Mario Day, and were once known for having performed way down the list at the famed Donnington Metal Fest. But by 1982 they had gone through the requisite number of lineup changes, and were financially hanging on by their fingertips. They decided on one last shot at the big time: a single. The A-side was a ditty called *Trickster*. The B-side was a roaring metal send up of *Hey Joe*. The upshot was that nobody cared, and More was soon no more. Hey, they can't all be happy endings!

More successful but equally obscure outside of the Communist Bloc world was a Slovenian/Yugoslavian prog rock outfit called Buldozer who, in between battles over ideology with stringent government regulations, managed a good 20-year run. *Hey Joe* came into the picture in 1982 when Buldozer released a mammoth two album live set entitled *Ako ste slobodni veceras* (*If You're Available Tonight*), which featured a progressive rock/metal/classical mash-up of *Hey Joe*, interspersed with such surreal elements as mock interview snippets with the band members talking about sex and drugs. File Buldozer under "For Special Tastes Only."

More often than not during the 80's, *Hey Joe* was an afterthought; added to an album as glorified filler by a band that, quite frankly, did not have enough original material. And at the other end of the spectrum there's Kiss who, it seems, have never done a song they could not turn a buck on. At a concert in Dusseldorf, Germany, on October 30, 1984, the band took time out from doing their set song list to break into a truly strange medley. First up was a lean and mean *Hey Joe,* which clocked in at 1:27 on the rock watch. As almost an afterthought, the band chimed in with a grab at *La Bamba*. Literally within days, Kiss struck a deal with European label IMC to put out a limited edition single in Spain entitled *1980's Ladies*. *Hey Joe* was the A-side.

Proving they were no slouches in the *Hey Joe* arena, The Who, on their 1989 world tour suddenly got it in their heads that they could do a decent take on Hendrix's *Hey Joe* live, and proved it at various stops on the tour. While the band, for whatever reason, never saw fit to include a live version or a studio version on any of their subsequent albums, the bootleg industry was all over the 1989 tour, and The Who's rendition of *Hey Joe.*

A live version of that *The Kids Are Alright Tour '89's* Texas stopover hit the bricks moments after the band left the stage. Likewise, another boot of The Who's Italian tour stop, entitled *Horton Hears The Who*, was not too far behind. A third illicit knockoff of a tour date featured *Hey Joe*, in this case chronicling the New York show and called *The Who: Night Before The Resurrection.* Aptly, this bootleg hid seemingly in a cave for a dozen years before emerging into the light in 2002.

Easily one of the most daring interpretations of *Hey Joe* in the 80's had to be the take by the late surrealist, multi- instrumentalist *Nash The Slash.* When he wasn't going all progressive and off the beaten path with his weapons of choice: the electric violin and mandolin, the bizarre pop star, who spent much of his career swathed in thick bandages to hide his identity, showcased a keen pop sensibility, and on his 1984 album *American Bandages*, turned his arsenal of pop sensibilities into a surprisingly up tempo and danceable *Hey Joe*. His take seemed to have a bit of everything: chunky techno elements, quasi/80's pop vocals and a nifty chorus sing along. *Nash The Slash's* music rarely received radio airplay, and it's a shame that his version of *Hey Joe*, oh so blatantly commercial, never found a home in radio's Top Ten. It's an undiscovered jewel that is brilliant in execution and style.

Soft Cell were not in the greatest place in 1983. The combination of fairly rampant drug use and an inconsistent second album had suddenly put the new wave/techno pop duo in a precarious critical situation. Enter *Hey Joe*, first as a B-side of a stalled single as part of a ditty called *Hendrix Medley,* and then, in 1984, on the album *The Art of Falling Apart*. As the introductory section to *Hendrix Medley*, Soft Cell's version of *Hey Joe* fairs fairly well, as a droning but not lazy instrumental tone interplays with Marc Almond's haunting and emotionless vocals.

In a somewhat less legal environment, Nick Cave & The Bad Seeds might never have crossed paths with *Hey Joe*, but when an originally scheduled studio album was stalled over a slight legal hiccup, and the mercurial Cave was working his well-documented psyche into a novel, the group compromised on what seemed a blatant stop gap album made up entirely of covers called *Kicking Against The Pricks*.

The surprise was that *Pricks* survived the tag of throwaway to become one of Nick Cave &The Bad Seeds most critically revered and darkly inventive albums, with particular kudos going to the cover of *Hey Joe*. From the onset, this *Hey Joe* was a minimalist wall of techno sound that tested the concept of tone and style as it pertained to the dark and desperate side of life. Cave's disembodied vocals over a suitably muddy mix came across as darkly foreboding, like an outtake of a *Morricone* spaghetti western movie passage. It was not so much an interpretation as it was a full on dare.

The mid-80's were also good times for *Hey Joe* obscurities and inanities that stretched around the world. Remember the French pop star Alain Bashung? I didn't think so. Well around the time Nick Cave and The Bad Seeds were racking up the huzzahs for their *Hey Joe*, Alain decided to do a French cover of the song based primarily on another French cover of it some 20 years previous, by Johnny Hallyday on his album *Live Tour 85*. Bashung's version barely registered a pulse, and even in France could only manage a feeble 59 on the French pop charts.

Hallyday's cover and the ensuing 'appropriated' writing credits would serve as a guide to just how publishers would go after those who were playing fast and loose with Billy Roberts' baby.

Bo Goldsen was President of Criterion Music Group in the late 60's, establishing a strong presence in France, and by the early 1970's had established a sub-publishing agreement with Billy Roberts' publisher Third Story Music. In a series of email conversations with this author, Goldsen acknowledged that Hallyday and *Hey Joe* were almost immediately in his sights.

"Our first order of business was to get the writer/publisher royalties back from Johnny Hallyday on his French adaptation of his recording of *Hey Joe*," explained Goldsen. "Hallyday had erroneously claimed both adaptation and lyric credits for his adaptation. My understanding at the time was that he recorded the song based on the Jimi Hendrix recording."

Goldsen recalled that Hallyday had not taken great pains to hide his deception. "Johnny openly took adapter's credit, so it was clearly on his label copy. It was all pretty cut and dried. Third Story Music had the right to reclaim the money as publisher, and included the writer's share—all the recovered royalties." With Jack Robinson from Criterion leading the legal wrangling, the company managed to retrieve all the money from Hallyday's publishing company, which included all performing rights money. "We did get all the money from Johnny's publishing company, and ended up getting all the money due Third Story. I know *Hey Joe* was a big hit for Johnny in France, and that the money involved was substantial."

It seemed inevitable that Weird Al Yankovic would take a swipe at *Hey Joe* at some point, and on the album *Weird Al Yankovic in 3-D* he would lay down some mighty accordion riffs in a snippet from *Polkas on 45* which, in its own way, made the song sound even more dangerous and demented—not to mention good for a few laughs.

During this period, *Hey Joe* was also making inroads into new places. The Pacific Northwest was already booming as a hotbed of emerging styles by the mid 80's, with pop, new wave, and grunge, bringing us through this odyssey of rock's little engine that could to a new wave/punk outfit called Dead Moon. Toody Cole's response of this author's unexpected ring up was in keeping with the way others had responded to interview requests: she laughed hysterically. Once she wiped the tears away, this better half of the husband/wife team of Fred and Toody, who piloted Dead Moon through much of the halcyon years of the Seattle scene, proved the ideal guide through her memories of *Hey Joe*.

"The first time I heard *Hey Joe* was when Fred's early band The Weeds was playing it," she recalled. "Fred's former band The Lollipop Shoppe [a short lived but unexpectedly influential band in the mid-60's] would play *Hey Joe* all the time, just like I'm sure every other band from the 60s did. Not everybody had a recorded version of *Hey Joe*, but everybody seemed to have a live version."

Dead Moon was formed in 1987, and began recording their first release, a seven-inch '45, the following year. That the band's debut single was made up of covers of *Parchment Farm* and *Hey Joe* was almost a given, recalled Toody. "When we first started Dead Moon, we were doing nothing but cover material. *Hey Joe* was one of those songs we had down pat and that we felt comfortable recording. When it came to recording our first full-length album, we were like most first album bands in that we did not have a lot of original material. So it was kind of like, 'Okay, we need to fill up these tracks.'"

Dead Moon's recording of *Hey Joe* was, typical of the day, quick and dirty. "We were always a one or two take band that recorded everything live off the floor. I would say recording that song took the better part of a day. Everybody always seemed to be trying to imitate what Hendrix did, but what we did was closer to The Leaves version. It was a little punky and a little faster."

And as it turned out, *Hey Joe* turned out to be Dead Moon's talisman. Word got around about the band and the song in Europe. A German record company stepped in and began releasing Dead Moon's music. And while Dead Moon would remain a curiosity in the states, the band was unexpectedly ordained gods overseas. "We started going to Europe in the 90's and didn't do our first US tour until 94," said Toody. "Europe just treated us like gods. They paid for our hotels and made sure we were getting fed each night. They treated us incredibly well and we started making incredible money over there. When we toured the US, it was get in your vans, spend all of your money on gas and then we were on our own as far as food and a place to stay. But the bottom line for all of that was that *Hey Joe* definitely got us going."

Dead Moon played *Hey Joe* live fairly regularly from 1987 to 1993. "We used to play it off and on live, but at some point we had so much original material that we pretty much phased the song out. But then every once in a while, somebody would request *Hey Joe* at a show, and so we would play it for old time sake."

Toody maintains a sense of respect for the song *Hey Joe*, and the impact it has had on generations of musicians. "It's important to have songs like *Hey Joe* become iconic. *Hey Joe* became much more after the fact than when it was first released."

By the 1980's, Billy Roberts, the man who had long ago been legally amended as the credited author of *Hey Joe*, was still very much alive and kicking. While his legal agents continued the often Herculean task of finding out who was illegally putting out *Hey Joe* under other than Robert's credit, the royalties continued to come Robert's way at a consistent and comfortable pace, but there would be no huge creative payoffs or other than token appreciation for the songwriter who had penned a classic.

Roberts' appearances continued to be primarily low key club and concert appearances in the San Francisco Bay Area. Roberts had become a Godfather of sorts, receiving signs of respect in the form of opening slots on shows by Steve Miller and Carlos Santana. His songs, especially *Hey Joe*, were rarely heard on anything resembling a popular radio station, but, for Roberts, his golden years had become comfortable. That his name could not be mentioned without some reference to *Hey Joe* seemed perfectly fine with him.

Such was the case on August 20, 1986, when a small San Francisco in-house jam at the local Club 9 bar, which featured such stellar local musicians as

Marc Shapiro

John Cippolina, Nick Gavenites, Greg Elmore and Dave Kilmer was joined on stage by Roberts. The impression by those in the audience was of a man quietly confident and shy. Over the course of his career, Roberts had gone on to write and recorded a long list of quite good folksongs. But he knew the primary reason he was there that night was to bask in the glory of his greatest hit. Roberts was reportedly introduced to the audience as being "a great songwriter. I think his biggest hit was a song that was recorded by a lot of people. That song was *Hey Joe*."

Chapter Nine

The 90'S Will Do

In the early 90's interest continued in *Hey Joe*, growing to such a degree that it was speculated superstars of legendary status were toiling in their studios to put an all-star stamp on renditions of *Hey Joe*, but seemed like a well-intended fairy tale, but there was no sense that there was any truth to the reports.

In reality a lot of different musicians, hailing from wildly different universes, had found a lot in the song that was suddenly worth their time. The Offspring, the then-reigning hardcore punk band, would end up tapping *Hey Joe* twice, first as part of their pre-fame 1991 EP *Baghdad*, and, in 1997, as the B-side of their single *Gone Away*. Both versions passed muster as speedy, mondo-aggresso punk sendups, well worth a listen, but ultimately nothing more than a spirited knock off.

A much smarter and deliberate version of *Hey Joe* surfaced in 1990 when the veteran reggae group Black Uhuru (formerly Uhuru), amid the chaos of a latest line- up change and teetering on the edge of finally disbanding, managed to creatively get it up one more

101

time with the album *Now*. They delivered a crisp amalgamation of *Hey Joe* influences, proving that there is nothing wrong with being straightforward. Black Uhuru's cover, equal parts dense reggae instrumentation and a subtle but electric nod to Hendrix, showed the band and the song as equal masters of emotion and the moment.

At this point in history, *Hey Joe* was getting a good, honest and muscular approach in the hands of a myriad set of musicians. *Hey Joe* had finally culminated into something that was being taken seriously. Finally, for the first time in a long time, a legend would come out to play.

More than a decade later, on January 22, 1992, *Axis Entertainment* rumored that Bob Dylan and original Hendrix Experience member Noel Redding, with and a couple of studio musicians, were heard blasting out covers of *Hey Joe* and a long lost Hendrix nugget entitled *Dignity* in an unnamed New York studio. That Dylan would choose to take on an out of character song like *Hey Joe* might seem gimmicky and exploitive. But by 1992 Dylan had transformed himself from somebody largely defined by past glories into a free-wheeling musical explorer. Who can forget the moment Dylan unexpectedly went electric and pissed off the diehard folkies back in the day? So yes, when it came to Dylan, anything was possible. By all accounts he was listening to everybody and everything and drawing all manner of influences and performers into his musical mix. As it would turn out, Dylan doing *Hey Joe* would, indeed, be evidenced in 1997 when an allegedly very good boot or an official promo release, *Lucky Not to Be Destroyed*, began making the rounds in France, as did an online concert video of Dylan doing *Hey Joe*.

Phillippe Rault, a renowned international record producer who had his own brush with *Hey Joe*, speculated to this author in a far reaching interview in 2016 that Dylan's inclination toward *Hey Joe* may well have come from crossing paths with long-revered rocker Willy DeVille. "I was struck by the look of Dylan in the 90's, which was very much the look that Willy DeVille was cultivating in those days. The hat, the goatee, the whole thing. I knew he had gone to see Willy perform a number of times. I'm sure Dylan was aware of *Hey Joe* from way back, but hearing Willy do it live might well have triggered an interest in the song again and got him to thinking, 'Maybe I should try this.'"

While the notion of a Dylan/Hendrix mash-up would be worth the ink on even a highly speculative level, *Axis Entertainment* took great pains to add legitimacy to the rumor that this actually occurred. Citing Glenn Dundas's authoritative *Tangled Up in Tapes: A Recording History of Bob Dylan*, the article expertly lays out the admittedly thin specifics of the tale. As to how this meeting between Dylan and Redding took place, we now turn to the vaults of The Howard Stern Show and a rarely heard interview done with Redding that his adventures at an after party commemorating the 30th Anniversary of The David Letterman Show, at which Dylan performed.

"Bob Dylan came in and sits down and we start talking," Redding elucidated in the Stern interview. "He asked me to play on a tune on his new album or something."

That 'something' would turn out to be a *Hey Joe* whodunit, the unnamed studio, the unnamed musicians, one of which may well have been Redding, and, finally the fact that this version has, as of this publishing, not been released on record. In fact, the Axis Entertainment story states that only time Dylan played *Hey Joe* in a live setting was at a July 12, 1992 concert in Juan Les Pins, France, in which Dylan, in typically reflective and defiant tones, belted out *Hey Joe* with the accompaniment of several named musicians, none of which are Redding. There is ample video evidence to support this.

Redding has not been among the living for some years now, and until Dylan's *Hey Joe* is finally put out for the masses or he deems it time to talk about that moment, the veracity of Redding's story, and this rumor, will be remain a mystery

At the other end of the spectrum, the song *Hey Joe* would prove a barometer for the career of soul-crooner Seal. Back in 1991 when Seal was barely a blip on the pop music screen, a powerful version of the song was on an EP released in the United Kingdom, to reviews that pretty much foretold his future. Flash forward to 1996. Seal had broken through to stardom, and one of the perks of the time was that the producers of the soundtrack for the movie *Set It Off* came to Seal with an open slot on the album. Knowing a good thing when he heard it, he dusted off a live version of *Hey Joe*, and that song, along with the power of the disc's other star performers, catapulted the album to Number Four on the *Billboard* album charts.

In a weird sort of cosmic connection, a somewhat altered arrangement of *Hey Joe* done up by doom metal band Type O Negative seemed a natural. But always smarter than the genre's stereotypes, TON had a couple of ideas up their sleeve. On the 1992 album *The Origin of The Feces*, *Type O Negative* retitled *Hey Joe "Hey Pete,"* in deference to the band's singer, grossed out the storyline to picture Joe/Pete as an unrepentant axe murder, and turned it into a multi-song concept. Type O Negative, a popular favorite on the doom/metal circuit, had long ago been crowned 'The Drab Four' by their legions of gore hounds. One listen to *Hey Pete* was all it took to confirm that the moniker was well-deserved.

Chapter Ten

Reconstructing *Hey Joe*

International record producer Phillippe Rault has a thing about important memories, and he's big on remembering the good stuff. "The first time I heard any version of *Hey Joe*? Tim Rose. 1966. Rose was in Europe on a promotional tour." For Rault, whose recording credits include the works of such legendary blues artists as Memphis Slim, Lightning Hopkins and Clarence Gatemouth Brown, his gut reaction was a spot on A. "I loved it. It had the drama. It was a totally different vibe. I didn't know The Leaves' version yet, and of course six months later the Hendrix version came through, and that was a huge, monster record."

Rault's admiration for *Hey Joe* would continue through the years, and in 1991 he became acquainted with the song on a professional basis, crossing paths with perennial critic's favorite, Willy DeVille. DeVille seemed destined to wear the yoke of 'critic's favorite' almost from the moment he formed the enigmatic, roots influenced group Mink DeVille in the early 1970's. The band immediately became a bit of 'a thing' on the strength of house band status at the punk emporium

CBGB's. DeVille was a 'heavy cat.' Jack Nitzsche, Dr. John, Mark Knopfler and Allen Touissant were drawn to his brand of roots rock that included accordion and strings, with a decidedly third world 'tude. Through numerous albums, DeVille remained a commercial stranger in his own land, never more than bubbling under on the *Billboard* charts, while slowly but surely establishing a more solid base in arts-friendly Europe.

By 1990, DeVille, who at the time was beginning to come out of a years' long battle with heroin, had finally seemed to find a home. A collection of soul and rhythm and blues tracks on a small New Orleans based label, entitled *Victory Mixtures*, sold surprisingly well in France and inspired French record label FNAC to take a chance on DeVille. "They asked me to put together an album for Willy in The States," remembered Rault. "Originally the album was going to be produced by Jack Nitzsche. But Nitzsche was not really in an operating state of mind in those days and, at that time, Willy was sort of vacillating himself."

Vacillating was putting it mildly. Over the years, DeVille had cultivated a rather intense dislike for Los Angeles, where the album *Backstreets of Desire* would be recorded. "I say that every time I record in Los Angeles that I'll never do it again, and I keep doing it," Deville ranted in an *Allmusic.com* interview. "I hate LA. It's the worst. I think they eat their children there."

Rault chose producer John Philip Shenale to handle the lion's share of the recording. "So they started working on the record. As it turned out, Willy was intent on recording a number of songs from previous recording sessions. He had a demo version of *Hey Joe* he had done sometime late in 1991 in New Orleans, just a three-piece band and himself. He presented the demo to me and said, 'I want to do this song.'"

Rault listened to the demo. His reaction? Lukewarm at best. "I listened to it and I told Willy 'You know, we've had so many versions of *Hey Joe* before. This doesn't really sound like a new take.' It was okay, but it didn't really bring much to the table. 'We really need to find some different way of doing this.'"

DeVille's response was " I really want to do this song."

For Rault, the challenge of *Hey Joe* gave him the opportunity to get hands on the project. "So I went to Phil [Shenale] and said 'I'm going to try and find something to do with *Hey Joe*.'"

Rault knew enough about DeVille to know that his musical interests were very much rooted in Latin and New York Puerto Rican styles. "He was always interested in anything Mexico, and was always fascinated by the idea of banditos and all that darker imagery."

Rault began thinking of *Hey Joe* as a Tex/Mex hybrid, before turning his attention to a more tradition bound genre. "I had worked with some people involved in a Mariachi festival, and there was a band I was acquainted with called Los Comparos. As it turned out these guys would play on a regular basis in Los Angeles at a restaurant called La Fonda. Those guys were particularly good, and I was familiar with the record they had done with Linda Ronstadt. I went down to the restaurant, heard those guys and said 'Wow!' Willy was in town preparing for the record, and I called him up and said 'We're going to have dinner, and you've got to hear these guys.' Willy heard them and he loved them. I said, 'This is the way we should do *Hey Joe*, Mariachi style,' and to take it away from anything that has ever been done. So I got in contact with the musicians and started getting the session together."

With the aid of Los Comparos leader Victor Manuel Villa, Rault laid out a template that would take the expectedness of a Mariachi based *Hey Joe* into what the producer described as "a different kind of vibe." It was a vibe that De Ville instinctively gravitated toward, as he explained in a conversation with *Canal Magazine*. "I wanted to get the song back to a place where it originally came from. Instead of doing something like Jimi Hendrix, which would have been a cliché, I tried to take it back to the way it must have originally sounded, which would be with Mariachis. I put a bit of Pachuco street talking on it, and I added a couple of verses of my own."

Rault describes the session at Track Studios as "kind of like the old days. We went in at 11:00 and clocked out at 2:00, and the thing was cut. Willy fell right into it. He went for it. There were no headaches or anything. We did one instrumental track while we were in the studio over Willy's guide vocal, and then Willy came back in and did the final vocal. Then I went back in with a Cuban percussionist and laid down some percussion, because that kind of instrumentation is something most mariachi bands don't have. "

Rault was candid in saying that great pains were taken to get DeVille through the session and his current round of vices. "Basically, Willy had quit heroin at that point, and unfortunately, [as it] often happens, he replaced one thing with another, and alcohol had become more of a problem than anything else while we were in the studio.

"But fortunately Willy was into the song, and that was something serious for him. Our attitude going into record *Hey Joe* was that we had to know exactly when you could go into the studio and get him to do things. There were certain times of the day [more] conducive to getting him to work and get things done than others. The *Hey Joe* sessions were in the morning, which were a bit early for him. He wasn't completely straight, but he was capable of doing what he had to do."

Hey Joe was intended to be an album cut. "But all of a sudden in France there was a resurgence of the whole Tex-Mex thing in terms of food and fashion. The guys at the record label went through the album and decided that *Hey Joe* was the song that they really wanted to push."

Hey Joe would go to Number One in France and Spain, and Rault recalled that the song did quite well in Germany and Holland, catapulting *Backstreets of Desire* to international hit status and revitalizing DeVille's long dormant standing as a star of note. "I don't know who was more surprised that *Hey Joe* became a hit, Willy or myself. It was probably both of us. Willy was always like, 'I always knew it was going to be a hit.' Frankly I had been around music long enough to know that if you throw a song out there, you have to expect it to come back and bite you in the ass. But I do remember walking out of the session and having a good feeling for it. Willy's guitar player came up to me and was saying 'Man! That's a hit!' All I could say was maybe."

Chapter Eleven

Hey Joe...Mondo Obscuro

The success of Willy DeVille's south of the border version of *Hey Joe* opened up a seemingly brave new world. To that point, with rare exception, those attempting to reinvent the song rarely strayed far from the song's 60s' roots. There were more Hendrix variations than one could shake a guitar neck at. Much of them were quite good, but a lot immediately fell to the ravaged roads of forgettable and predictable.

The popularity of Hendrix's version of the song would also succeed in muddying its historical lineage. Most people were under the impression that the life of *Hey Joe* began with Hendrix, forgetting the history that spawned it.

Hey Joe had plateaued by the decade of the 90's. The song, after three decades in the public consciousness, had finally arrived in a state of grace. It had both the musical and street cred. Some bemoaned the fact that the legitimate song about an unrepentant premeditated murder was now on the verge of slipping over into mainstream, polite society. Supermarket openings and weddings could not be far behind. For better or worse, *Hey Joe* had become comfortable.

However, those even remotely familiar with the story of the song were well aware that *Hey Joe* could be the musical equivalent of a rattlesnake, hiding complacent in the musical weeds, but always poised to strike under the right circumstances. And so while *Hey Joe* activity had seemingly gotten quiet, it was far from slithering into its hole for good.

Musicians in the early 90's had gotten braver, and were making daring moves in the direction of the song as a legitimate piece of music rather than a dottering old chestnut, and were moving in many subtle, divergent and creative directions with it.

One of the more clever approaches to *Hey Joe* took place in 1992, when veteran blues and country slide guitar picker Jerry Douglas chose to work out the song on the album *Slide Rule*. Douglas's effort provided a darkly introspective and subtly disturbing approach to the song that added a depth that straight ahead rock and pop versions could not approach. Douglas definitely struck a chord with *Hey Joe* that is worth a nuanced listen.

In 1992, Buckwheat Zydeco, known primarily for his Louisiana/down home blend of danceable soul and blues, threw a curve of sorts when he recorded *Hey Joe* as a heavily Hendrix-influenced brand of funk on his album *On Track*. In light of the rampant experimentation going on at the time, Buckwheat Zydeco worked in the present while looking to the past.

Ted Fox, Buckwheat Zydeco's long time manager and producer, recalled in a 2016 interview with the author, that when it came to bringing out the truth in *Hey Joe*, Buckwheat walked the walk. "Buck grew up dirt poor in the middle of Louisiana: twelve brothers

112

and sisters in two rooms. If they didn't go out and shoot something they didn't have anything to eat. Everyone in his neighborhood was carrying a gun, or was in prison for 40 years. I would say that Buck's version of *Hey Joe* was the most understandable and legitimate of any version. A 16-year old kid from the suburbs singing those lyrics was an affectation. Buck lived the kind of life in *Hey Joe*."

Fox recalled that in 1992 Buckwheat had signed to the über-hip Island Records, so in an attempt to add more rock influences he brought *Hey Joe* to Buck's attention prior to going into the studio to record *On Track*. "Of course he knew the song. He knew the Hendrix stuff even though it was not necessarily what he grew up listening to. At that point, he could play *Hey Joe* in his sleep."

Fox related that his style of producing the *Hey Joe* session was simple. "What Buck did and what I hoped he would do was to take that chestnut of a song and make it his own. He made it a dramatic, meaningful, rocking song. Whether he was doing his accordion solo or his Hammond B3 solo, 20 years later his version of *Hey Joe* still makes the hair on the back of my neck stand up. The session didn't take long. He basically went in and killed it."

As good as Buckwheat Zydeco's version of *Hey Joe* was, it would pale in sheer ferocity to the version offered up in the mid 90's by the Black heavy metal band Bodycount. Bodycount, fronted by the notorious Ice T who brought the song *Cop Killer* kicking and screaming into the world, offered up a version up of *Hey Joe* that was so Hendrix influenced that you'd swear the ghost of Jimi was lurking somewhere in the shadows.

You can find Bodycount's rough and raw *Hey Joe* on two albums, the band's 1993 LP *Born Dead*, and 1994's *Stone Free: A Tribute To Jimi Hendrix*.

Into the 90's, *Hey Joe* had always seemed the domain of the more serious minded musician. But, as exhibited by Cher, there were those who occasionally took to *Hey Joe* in an attempt to gather street cred by doing the song, usually dolled up in their signature style. By the early 90's, Eddie Murphy had joined the club, trying real hard to add "pop star" to his already top drawer acting credentials, and, as it turned out, with some success. But even his most ardent 'yes' men had to swallow hard when Murphy informed them that a track on his 1993 album, *Love's Alright*, would be his interpretation of *Hey Joe*.

Murphy's version would be Hollywood faux earnest, a by-the-numbers Hendrix workout, coupled with the amusing aside of Murphy's vocals straining to be believable. But let's give the devil his due: Murphy knew his audience dwelt on the pop side, and was not about to batter their senses with anything too dark and foreboding. So Murphy managed the feat of turning *Hey Joe* into something non-threatening for the masses that would be good for the bottom line. Next.

Up a few notches from Eddie Murphy's effort was the rollicking good time that was Captain Sensible's live take on *Hey Joe* on his 1994 solo live album *Live from The Milky Way*. Captain Sensible, whose day job was founding member of the legendary punk band The Damned, turned in a rollicking good time of a *Hey Joe*, as befitting the concert atmosphere, and gave a lighthearted, reckless sheen to the song's normal somber tones.

A true oddity but one well worth listening to was

Hey Joe, courtesy of the mid 90's Celtic/folk/rock London band *Lick The Tins*—that is if you can imagine *Hey Joe* reimagined as an Irish jig. The song is a light speed instrumental, heavy on Celtic instrumentation and, by degrees, almost impossible to recognize as *Hey Joe*. Their version appeared on their one and only album, *Blind Man on a Flying Horse*, but if you're looking for a fun, harmless take on *Hey Joe*, you could do a lot worse.

Guitar Shorty's 1996 take on *Hey Joe* on the album *Billy Jean Blues* is not something that jumps out at the listener as anything more than a competent cover of Hendrix. But with repeated listenings it becomes apparent that the veteran blues guitarist knows the basics and what it takes to make the song shine. There's a sense of familiarity and tradition in Shorty's version, which, when coupled with his hypnotic sense of style and playing, is an enticing listen. It also bears repeating that Shorty sprang from the right side of the *Hey Joe* family tree, as he is Hendrix's brother-in-law.

Sisters of Mercy, hardly known as a good time party group, had made their reputation on the strength of introspective, pessimistic, and just plain bummer goth rock, which, when you think about it, could fit the vibe of *Hey Joe* to a T. When the band chose to include their *Hey Joe* in a live setting during a 1984 tour, their take was surprisingly straight forward and crisp, albeit a shade on the dour side: a good version to use to hide in a corner and shut out the world. It would take six years for a larger audience to get a taste of Sisters of Mercy's *Hey Joe*, on a record whose origin and legality have been somewhat in question, *Echoes Vol. 2*.

The Red Hot Chili Peppers, it can be argued,

normally have their shit together when it comes to their music and its presentation, but the band does seem to have this thing about *Hey Joe.* When it comes to getting the song down for any kind of posterity, they have a hard time remembering the lyrics. Or so it seems.

For a live show that ultimately went the bootleg route under the title *Flea's Birthday Party,* released in 1996 on the *Midnight Beat* label, the band managed only 52 seconds of the song before dissolving into a primitive audience sing-a-long that proved the audience did not know the lyrics either. Ten years later the band would once again attempt going the distance for the words to *Hey Joe* during a rehearsal session for the television series *Live From Abbey Road.* This time the Chili Peppers manage one minute and ten seconds of *Hey Joe* before packing it in.

Los Lobos had little problem remembering the words to *Hey Joe*. The Los Angeles based band has had *Hey Joe* in their crosshairs for a long time, and although they've never laid down the song in a studio setting, they have left ample traces of the song along the bootleg trail. In 1999-2000 alone, three recordings of *Hey Joe* in concert have been discovered in the underground boot-traders network.

Easily the most adventurous take on *Hey Joe* to rise out of the early to mid-90's was a truly obscure and gender bending version of *Hey Joe* entitled *Hey Joan* by Dutch pop singer Mathilde Santing. What could have easily been dismissed as a gimmick is actually a reasonably good take, in which Santing's low key and slightly whispery tones, coupled with the notion of the woman as killer, make for a less obvious and more thoughtful *Hey Joe.*

Chapter Twelve

Otis Loves *Hey Joe* Long Time

Otis Taylor is one of those straightforward blues cats. Taylor, who matter-of-factly boasts of jamming with Hendrix when he was barely legal, and is notorious for going off on a tangent at the drop of a hat, is not above being up front and apologetic at the end of a 2015 interview with this author on the ins and out of being up close and personal with *Hey Joe*.

"I'm sorry I don't have more to say about it [*Hey Joe*]," he chuckles. "I've recorded it three times, which I guess is sort of unusual for a person to do. The first album I ever did had *Hey Joe* on it. My biggest selling album had *Hey Joe* on it, and my most recent album *Hey Joe Opus*...well you get the picture. So it's sort of like there's a history with the song and me. I'm just a blues guy, but my history with the song is very strong."

The history, dare we say it—obsession, goes back quite a long way for Taylor. As a very young and quite talented youngster in the mid-60's, Taylor first heard *Hey Joe* as played by the band Love. His reaction? "Because I'm black I thought it was kind of funky," he recalled. "This was before all the hippies came along.

The song was interesting for me because the black guys weren't playing soul. They were playing rock."

Knowing how profound and to-the-gut the lyrics to *Hey Joe* are, Taylor admits to being at a loss for any deep interpretation back then. "Lyrics? I don't know. I was just a young kid. I wasn't that deep. He killed his girl and he ran off to Mexico. He killed his girl and he didn't want to die. It didn't shock me. I was playing old time funk music, which was all pretty much all cloak and dagger anyway."

In 1967, Taylor heard Jimi Hendrix's version of *Hey Joe*. Hendrix was an acquired taste at that point, and for the aspiring blues man, his version did not go down easily. "When I first heard Hendrix's version I didn't like it as much. I thought it was kind of strange. But, like everything else, I guess I just had to get used to it. The more I got into Hendrix, the more I got used to it [*Hey Joe*]."

The mercurial Taylor stepped away from music sometime in the mid 70's, and spent the next 19 years living the life of an antiques dealer. But he got the itch again in 1995, and returned to a career in music, where he was once again reunited with *Hey Joe*. "When I made my comeback around '95. I wrote a few songs, but in those days to play out you needed enough music for a full set, and so we had to come up with some covers, and that included *Hey Joe*."

At that time, Taylor was developing a sound that has often been described as 'trance music,' with no small amount of jazz/classical and psychedelic influences thrown in for good measure. Taylor playing live in the 90's must have been a truly 'different' experience, especially, he recalls, when it came to *Hey Joe*.

"At the time we were a band that did not use a drummer," he chuckles. "The band was simply guitar and bass. Plus, when it came to *Hey Joe*, I didn't play an A chord like everybody else does. Playing [my] way always gave me a different feeling. My head is in a different place than Hendrix's when it comes to *Hey Joe*."

Taylor ventured into the recording studio for the first time in 1996 with the album *Blue Eyed Monster*, an album whose mixture of covers and originals was the logical extension of what Taylor had been doing since returning to music and one that was, in the least, unorthodox.

"I didn't play any guitar on *Blue Eyed Monster*. And to be perfectly honest, I never knew the lyrics to *Hey Joe*. My memory was real bad when it came to song lyrics, and when it came to *Hey Joe*. I would learn a couple of lyrics, and that's all I would use. I'm sure whatever words I used on *Hey Joe* were different, as I tended to change the words to songs all the time. I didn't really sing on *Blue Eyed Monster*. Nowadays I don't give a shit. I can say whatever I want."

What Taylor wanted for *Hey Joe* on his 2008 album *Recapturing The Banjo* was an intricate wall of sound in which banjo and Taylor's patented six string guitar style collided in a sonic trip which pays homage to the traditional values that came before, while ranging far and wide on new frontiers. Yes, I'm waxing poetic, but, in Taylor's hands, it seems justified.

"At the end of the day *Hey Joe* is just a cool song," Taylor says, with legitimate admiration. "I've been playing *Hey Joe* for 19 years, so I've never really stopped playing it. Whenever I do a concert people expect to hear it."

The fact that *Hey Joe* is inexorably tied to Taylor's work is very much in evidence in his 2015 release *Hey Joe Opus Red Meat*, a very dark magnum opus in which *Hey Joe* bookends a literal loop of moody, thickly layered passages from a very 'other' place. "*Hey Joe Opus* is kind of psychedelic and classical. It's very jazzy. The album has a real sense of history between the song and myself. It's like a whole journey. The music never stops."

Despite the musical chances taken, Taylor laughs at the notion that the musician and the song sometimes go at loggerheads. In a 2014 documentary entitled *I Am Ali*, a snippet of *Hey Joe* plays under a scene that is credited at the documentaries' end crawl to Jimi Hendrix. "Well, I recently had it brought to my attention that the snippet of the song is actually my version, and so Hendrix is getting credit for my work. The irony is that while *Hey Joe Opus* is getting a lot of positive press, it's because everybody is crediting the song as being Hendrix's in reviews and such. I'm getting all this press because people think it's a Hendrix song, and, as your research indicates, a number of people did the song before Hendrix. But I'm not going to let it bother me. "*Hey Joe* is just what I do," he concluded. "The good thing is that I don't do it Hendrix's style. So at least I can't get sued."

Chapter Thirteen

Got *Hey* If You Want It

The Flowerz, with the exception of having a rare for the time girl drummer, were no better or worse than the myriad garage bands that popped up like weeds in the 60s, in the wake of the success of Hendrix and Leaves' versions of *Hey Joe*. The band, who favored early Small Faces and The Who in their repertoire, had a couple of very local hits on the miniscule Kingston label before disbanding very late in the 60's. A youthfully earnest *Hey Joe* showcased basic chops, and was not better than okay by garage band standards.

That should have been end of story. The reason why they're making their appearance this far along the chronology was that, in 1998, the band's all covers album from back in the day, *Flyte*, was remixed and rereleased some 30 years later on Arf Arf Records. This new offering, like the band, is so-so at best, but if you're looking for a cheap thrill and you look really hard, there's a long lost video out there of The Flowerz performing *Hey Joe* in a backyard concert that features typical teen angst and an audience of questionably legal teens consuming adult beverages.

On the surface, the late 90's were shaping up as a retrenching period for *Hey Joe*. Everybody was still doing it, but there was nothing that really jumped out and made you say wow!...

...Until O' Rappa's brutal and telling take on *Hey Joe* on their 1996 album *Rappa Mundi*. O'Rappa, a tough-minded Brazilian reggae/rock band that was not above throwing rap, funk and hip hop into the mix, conjured up a truly threatening version that took defiant steps away from the traditional storyline and into a modern day gang and gun soaked world, where a haunting refrain of 'Hey Joe where you going with that gun in your hand?' plays out against an angry apocalyptic world view. Creepy on its own, but when seen with some particularly tough-minded videos that have accompanied the song over the years, this is a *Hey Joe* that will keep you up nights.

The punk rock band Fifteen is nowhere near as ominous as O'Rappa. Their 1996 version of *Hey Joe* on the album *No Place Like Home (Good Night)* contains the requisite angst, but it is also an example of what happens when you stray too far from the source material. Fifteen's version is anchored by a nice, crunchy riff. The vocals are a whole other story, so buried behind the musical bash as to make them largely indecipherable, except for the 'Hey Joe where you going with that gun in your hand.' Fifteen is an example of how not everybody who has attempted *Hey Joe* has gotten it right.

Here's one fans might easily have missed. In 1996 a whole bunch of cool people from cool groups got together for a bash about on an album entitled *Yardbirds Experience: British Thunder*, a quite solid workout on

Yardbirds, Zeppelin and other rock classics. Of particular interest in this recording, which features Jim McCarty of The Yardbirds, Noel Redding of The Jimi Hendrix Experience, Eddie Phillips of Creation, Ray Phillips of The Nashville Teens, Matthew Fisher of Procol Harum, Phil May of Pretty Things and Ray Major of Mott the Hoople, is a three song Hendrix medley that kicks off with *Hey Joe* and some nifty guitar pyrotechnics courtesy of Phillips, adding credence to the notion of how good and influential Creation might have been in Hendrix's world.

Six degrees of The Grateful Dead, as it pertained to *Hey Joe*, would once again surface in 1996. In itself that was not too surprising. The Dead and their countless offshoots and solo projects would often include some aside to *Hey Joe* at some point, and have nearly always been difficult to pin down. Well, here's one we know for sure: *At the Further Jam* in 96, former *Dead* member Bob Weir teamed with the band Ratdog for a rousing rendition of *Hey Joe*.

A band that seemingly came out of nowhere and truly got it right when it came to *Hey Joe* was a post-punk Washington D.C. group called The Make Up. The Make Up had a socialist, bordering on communist philosophy about things. Musically it was an immediately enticing mixture of gospel, pop, rock and funk. By the time they entered the studio for what would be their final album, 1999's *Save Yourself*, The Make Up were all in when it came to their version of *Hey Joe*.

Hey Joe, in their hands, literally had everything: an introspective intro and a crisp looking inward attitude, and a slight, but clever spoken-word exchange between Joe and the woman everybody assumes is the ghost of the person he killed, begging Joe to come back from Mexico and be with her. As Joe's decision wavers, the song suddenly breaks into all slam, bam guitar bash that finally fades out with the song. The Make Up never made it big, but with this *Hey Joe*, they certainly went out with a bang.

Little more than a very good footnote in the *Hey Joe* book of days, but worth a mention, is German heavy metal guitarist Axel Rudi Pell. Pell's take, which appeared initially as a bonus track on the Japanese version of his 1999 album *Black Moon Pyramid* before finding a home on his album *The Ballads II* the same year, is a daring bit of business. After a very short vocal intro, Pell goes into a cut-long jam, much in the wheelhouse of Hendrix. Points should be awarded for what is an all-instrumental version of *Hey Joe* that won't put you to sleep, and is a fairly tight tutorial for anyone aspiring to a degree of Rock God status.

Of some note was the fact that Tim Rose came out of a self-imposed ten-year hiatus from music, during which he had earned a degree or two and worked in such exotic jobs as construction worker and Wall Street stockbroker. Upon his return to the music scene, Rose found that he still had some heavy friends and a certain amount of cache, especially in the UK. Among those musicians was Nick Cave. Cave and Rose became fast friends, and Rose would end up opening for Cave in several high profile London concerts.

Rose's newfound acceptance in hip music circles would result in the singer releasing the first album in a dog's age, 1997's *Haunted*, a highly evocative collection of older material recorded live, along with some newer material. Of particular interest was Rose's rendition of *Hey Joe*, done under the long ago alternative title *"Blue Steel .44."*

His renewed acceptance late in life mellowed the often-taciturn Rose, who had been notorious for, among other things, downplaying Hendrix's version of *Hey Joe*. In an interview in *Tim Rose The Musician.com*, Rose softened on that subject. "Since my version of *Hey Joe* was never released as a single, I don't think it would have hurt me at that point for Hendrix to release it. It so happens that Hendrix had a hit with *Hey Joe* which people connected with me, and so it was useful to my career."

Finally it wouldn't be the 90's without Helge Schneider (a/k/a Helge and The Fire Fuckers). Helge Schneider, another German with a thing for *Hey Joe*, is a Renaissance man: musician, comedian, author, and actor. On his 1999 album *Eiersalat In Rock*, Schneider, aided and abetted by the very tight Fire Fuckers, offered up *Hey Joe* complete with flamboyance and laughs, as a very legitimate, faster-than-the-speed-of-sound stomp that is equal parts polka and the best instrumental moments of the US band The Outlaws. It took me one listen to get beyond the jokiness of it all. By the time I got through listen two and three, I was hooked.

And I still can't stop laughing.

Chapter Fourteen

2001: A *Hey Joe* Odyssey

And now for something completely different.

Imagine, if you will, a melodic, oh so cool, oh so mellow jazz take on *Hey Joe*, courtesy of the experimental jazz fusion trio Medeski, Martin and Wood on their 2000 live release *Tonic*. Now imagine *Hey Joe* over a candlelight dinner with your woman (or man) in a smoky jazz dive. It's all instrumental, so there will be no lyrics popping up to destroy the mood.

On the surface, Medeski, Martin and Wood are not the typical exponents of *Hey Joe*. Together for more than 25 years, none of the members had ever played *Hey Joe* until very late in the 1990's, and its inclusion in the live album *Tonic* was the first time it was recorded by them in any way. They seemed to be too ivory tower-inclined to be getting their hands dirty with such a ruffian of a song. In conversation, Medeski admitted that he was a babe in the woods when it came to *Hey Joe*.

"I heard Hendrix's version when I was a kid," he recalled. "At the time I don't remember having any strong feelings about the song. It never struck me as odd that somebody would be singing about killing his old lady and then running off to Mexico. For me, the song has always been a kind of deep, dark blues. But when I was in high school I was all into jazz, and didn't really get Hendrix or *Hey Joe*. Finally I got more mature and I started to get it. But nobody in this band had ever played *Hey Joe*…"

…Until around 2000.

"We had reached a point where we had been playing a lot of rock clubs and big concert arenas," said Medeski. "We had become a part of the whole jam band scene, and had just opened for Dave Mathews. But we were beginning to question what we were doing musically. The scene was all rock and roll and partying, and that was starting to lose its appeal. We had been doing this for a long time, and so we decided that we needed to get back to our roots."

Going back to their roots meant going all acoustic and ditching microphones on stage, related Medeski. "We had always done covers, old jazz standards and things like Bob Marley. So when I suggested *Hey Joe* to the rest of the band, it was an easy sell. We all felt there was something we could do with the song. Hendrix's version was loud and rocking. When we got *Hey Joe*, we felt we could do something with it as a ballad. We didn't have the lyrics, so we felt we could give it a deeper sense of melancholy. Instrumental music is a language all its own in terms of how it expresses things, and we felt *Hey Joe* was the perfect song to interpret that language in a way that the words can't."

Medeski, a deep and often abstract musical thinker, made his points on how they changed the *Hey Joe* vibe from raucous to mellow in broad strokes.

"There was nothing easy or difficult about it. We had already played it live quite a bit, so we instinctively knew where we were going with the song. It was kind of brush strokes to paint the landscape: the six basic chords and a blues and soulful cadence. We definitely pulled *Hey Joe* to a jazz place, even though the song is not really jazz…"

… "It just came out. It just happened."

The more experimental progress side of *Hey Joe*, coupled with emerging musical styles from seemingly unexpected sources, continued to be a favorite amalgamation in the early part of the decade. In particular, international artists, many seemingly miles removed from the basic nature of the song and the vibe that had been American in origin, were beginning to take their creative swings.

Of particular note is Italian composer/musician Franco Battiato. Known primarily in Europe, and largely a favorite in classical circles, Battiato was a creative of the times, and by 2001 was moving into pop, new wave and other progressive sounds and notions. Consequently, many critics were taken aback when, on his 2001 album *Ferro Battuto*, he turned the expected raw, crushing vibe of *Hey Joe* into an instrumental operatic lullaby, very easy on the ears, driven by subtle keyboard and synthesizer runs and a leisurely pace. Once the lyrics were out of the equation, it appeared that *Hey Joe* could be something socially acceptable and something quite capable of rocking your baby to sleep at night.

One would not think that Robert Plant, by 2002, would have had any further worlds to conquer. But there was a bit of trepidation surrounding the album

Dreamland, and, for our purposes, the inclusion of the song *Hey Joe*. *Dreamland*, made up primarily of covers, was Plant's first solo album in nine years and his first with a new band, The Strange Sensation. When it came to his version of *Hey Joe*, Plant wisely chose a middle ground, with only a hint of Led Zeppelin's monsters of metal bravado and often over-cooked drama. In its stead, we discover a multi-tiered arc of moodiness, and a haunting quality resolving in a fiery wind-down at the end: a superior approach on all counts.

If you're looking to win a bar bet and/or start a fight, here's a bit of *Hey Joe* lore from 2002 that might result in one, or both. On September 7, 2002, Stephen Stills, along with former Hendrix band members Mitch Mitchell and Billy Cox participated in one of many all-star tributes to Jimi Hendrix at the annual San Diego Street Scene music festival. It is said that Stills, Mitchell and Cox did a pile driver version of *Hey Joe* in front of what was reportedly 100,000 witnesses. There are several Hendrix completist websites that mention the show in some detail, and even offer the day's lineup. But while the urban legends of rare tapes being passed back and forth persist, there are no actual recordings—including bootlegs—that exist on even the clandestine market. At least not yet.

If any version of *Hey Joe* truly invigorated and inspired the potential of both the song in the early to mid-2000's, it would have to be the near-perfect jazz-fueled workout of Vijay Iyer with his rendition *Because of Guns (Hey Joe Redux)*, off the equally arresting concept album that spawned it, 2003's *Blood Sutra*. This is a take that captures and reinvents styles as it grows from a sturdy, stark piano introduction to a living, breathing presence that, by song's end, plows a mash up of bass, drum and horns into a rising, fiery crescendo. In a space of seven minutes and change, this version singlehandedly gives *Hey Joe* new life. Excuse me for getting all high and mighty here, but versions like this truly inspire.

The mid 2000's also saw its share of good, but not ultimately exceptional, takes on *Hey Joe*. Bryant Bjork, known for his work in the stoner metal band *Kyuss* and a fixture on the Palm Desert music scene, offered up a slow and meandering cover on his 2004 album *Local Angel* that was passable, but lacking in the passion department. The Gabe Dixon Band, a Miami group that made some noise before finally disbanding, put out a version of *Hey Joe* on their 2005 live EP *Live At World Café*. It's a rendition that might have been decent if it had not been betrayed by a poor sound system that buried the vocals and all the other instruments, save for some sturdy and audible piano work.

Is there not room for serious exploitation in the highly charged world of *Hey Joe*? Try this one on for size: *Hey OJ* by a Utah based group called Altamont Speedway. On the surface, it's so obvious it's laughable. The title hauntingly splashes itself across a surprisingly decent Hendrix rock/blues bedding of sound. Ultimately the joke is on you, because not only is *Hey OJ* a good version, once you get past the gimmickry, but the whole album (*Vegan Stew*), occasional questionable sound quality aside, is okay-with-a-capital-O. And yes I did listen to enough of this puppy to insure myself a place in the seventh circle of hell.

Somewhere in between, where the middle ground teeters between good and okay, lies Majek Fashek, a quite good reggae/pop performer who gained a reputation internationally by the time he released his 2005 album *Rainmaker*, which included a fairly spirited version of *Hey Joe*. Its pop instrumentation and surprisingly upbeat and danceable passages, as well as muted vocals, made for a decent dance club tune. But *Hey Joe* would be Majek Fashek's last hurrah. Not long after the album's release the singer went into a deadly spiral of divorce, drugs and homelessness that ended with Majek Fashek winding up in rehab. There might be a song in all this. Maybe it could be called *Hey Majek*.

Chapter Fifteen

Class In Session: Your Instructor Vernon Reid

Vernon Reid recently wandered into a New York City club. It was hip, pretty much packed and, on that particular day, a regularly scheduled jam session was in progress. Suddenly a group of musicians, with a female singer at the helm, broke into a version of *Hey Joe.* Reid, best known as the founder of the African American heavy metal band Living Color, was immediately drawn in. It was not like the song was new to him. He had been hearing *Hey Joe* since the early 70's, and had played it many times over the years. But the way this woman laid *Hey Joe* out there was unexpected and electrifying, and it immediately brought back in a rush, his reasons why he loved the song.

"*Hey Joe* is an amazing song," recalled Reid, warming to the conversation in 2016. "Anyone who is into Jimi Hendrix, *Hey Joe* is one of those turns. You have to play *Hey Joe*. For me, *Hey Joe* has always been a deeply problematic song in a lot of ways. It's fascinating. It's one of those songs, like *House of The Rising Sun*. It's a really interesting American artifact."

Reid is a deep thinker, one who, intellectually strives for every possible angle on a subject. He can be philosophical, quick with a theory or notion, and deadly serious, with some subtle humor, when exploring a subject. He can be the equivalent of a learned college professor if a subject strikes his fancy. And when it comes to *Hey Joe*, class is definitely in session.

"The first time I heard *Hey Joe*, it was sometime after Hendrix had passed," recalled Reid, whose reverence for the Hendrix version becomes obvious as the conversation continues. "It was in the early 70's, when the passing of Hendrix was still like a raw wound in rock and roll, and radio was playing Hendrix a lot, especially *Hey Joe*."

Like many, the then teenage Reid thought, "*Hey Joe* is a cool song." But he also related how his gut reaction to the song went a lot deeper than the cool factor. "I remember thinking to myself that the song was very interesting. I didn't think about the morality of the song at all. But I did recognize that it struck me as a great story, with the emphasis on the story."

Musically, Reid dissected the song as being much more than a simple rock song. "It's not the blues. It's more of a folk narrative. Hendrix partially took the influence of Bob Dylan and transmogrified it into *Hey Joe*. It's kind of rhythm and blues. It's a funny song. It's a narrative in which the protagonist is telling the listener why he did what he did. There's also a sense of transformation. At the end of the day it's a soundtrack to a man that's on the run."

Reid's thoughts once again return to the recent live performance and how the singer's rough, feminine perspective triggered a notion as to how he would record *Hey Joe*. "I've never recorded a version of *Hey Joe*. It's not that I was intimidated at the prospect. I've bored people to death with this, but I always felt that *Hey Joe* should be done with two vocalists. *Hey Joe* is a dialogue. It's always been the legitimate form of a male duet. *Hey Joe* is a song where you can easily have a dialogue with two different characters. I'm surprised that no one has really done the song that way."

Reid's coming of age as a *Hey Joe* devotee was late in the 70's. "I was jamming and learning at the feet of musicians like Andy LaSalle and Larry Marston. What I learned was that Hendrix's version of the song seemed to have been constructed with its own kind of logic. I always turned to Hendrix. *Hey Joe* to me is the way he moved the guitar chords, the chromatics of the sound and the construct of the riffs. There's an epic quality in what he did with the song. It's very relatable."

Reid also acknowledged that, early on, he felt out the cinematic quality of the song. "I connected with the song as being about the man with no name in the spaghetti westerns. The song is very much a spaghetti western because when the guy says 'I'm going down to Mexico', well, I'm thinking that he's going down to Mexico on a horse. *Hey Joe* has a very traditional feel to it. It's always felt like an old tale. The song has no context in terms of time and space. Joe could have been a dude in Chicago. There's also the idea that the song is quite chilling in its premeditation."

That *Hey Joe* has survived in the public consciousness for the better part of five decades, and with the current climate of violence abroad in the land, Reid easily slides into a serious tone in describing *Hey Joe* in terms of today. "Hey Joe is a lot of things, but if you think of the song in terms of now, the song is also really disturbing. It kind of codifies violence against women as a viable option. I'm really open to the honesty of *Hey Joe*. But violence against wives and girlfriends is a fucking epidemic. It's not cute."

In the context of the song as it relates to now, Reid insists that the dark and disturbing side of *Hey Joe* has to be brought into the conversation. "The one thing that bothers me about *Hey Joe* is that the friend doesn't talk his friend out of doing it. Joe has the gun in his hand, and he's going down to shoot his old lady. Joe is not worried about being caught with a firearm. His friend isn't afraid of being shot, himself."

Reid concedes that the sentiment expressed by *Hey Joe* is also speaking to another time when people regularly took the law into their own hands. "It's about the commission of a crime, and it's also about getting away with the crime. In this day and age *Hey Joe* is asking a lot of legal, moral and ethical questions that are just being pushed in our faces."

Reid offers up one more reality check. "It's still a great song, but it is a song that is in our face in a lot of ways, because when the song came out 50 years ago we weren't as engaged as we are now. These days we kind of can't not ask those questions."

As the conversation winds down, things get a bit less heavy. Reid reiterates that a version of *Hey Joe*, done with two male vocalists, could be something striking, and perhaps, significant. He also laughingly offers up what would be the ideal follow up to *Hey Joe*:

"Joe winds up in Mexico. He's thrown in jail. He's on death row and, at the last possible minute, [he's extradited to] the United States…to stand trial."

Marc Shapiro

Chapter Sixteen

Random Stuff...But *Hey Joe*

Every once in a while a version of *Hey Joe* comes along that is neither fish nor fowl: not quite ready for serious consideration, but far too interesting to be dismissed out of hand. Such is the case with the 2006 release by rapper Big B on his album *Big B Presents: Random Stuff*. In Big B's quite capable hands, his *Hey Joe* is all over the place. Alternately ethereal with solid floating ease, and then fairly crunching with Hendrix-style guitar licks. While both sides of Big B are a better than average *Hey Joe* take, the haunting mellow side is easily the superior tone: one of those *Hey Joes* worthy of the occasional listen.

It doesn't get any more basic and to the point than *Hey Joe,* the ultimate punk mash by the oldest running punk band on the planet, UK's The Vibrators. On their 2006 album *Garage Punk*, and clocking in at five minutes and change, this is the way punk used to be back in the day—and still occasionally is: loud, brash, faster than the speed of sound with lots of defiant vocals, screaming guitars and a generally pissed off vibe. Just the good stuff.

Vibrators' drummer John 'Eddie' Edwards has a pretty good handle on *Hey Joe*. Old enough to be the only original member of the band which formed in the mid 70's, Edwards clearly remembers the time, especially as the song pertains to the United Kingdom. "The first time most people in England heard *Hey Joe* was the Hendrix version in 66-67," he related in a phone conversation during the band's 2016 US tour. "It was very bluesy to the people who heard it. Then we started hearing all these other, more aggressive versions coming over from America. But in England, it was known as Hendrix's first single."

Edwards remembers the first time he heard *Hey Joe* as being a seminal personal moment. "I thought 'Yeah, great.' It was a very good song. It had some interesting lyrics about killing your girlfriend and all that. It wasn't a pretty, sweet love song."

The opportunity to record *Hey Joe* came in 2006 when Cleopatra Records asked The Vibrators to do an album of classic garage band covers. The band sifted through countless garage band songs. We jumped at the chance because that was our roots and our kind of stuff....And, at some point, *Hey Joe* pops up. We wanted to do it because we thought it was a cool song. *Hey Joe* was kind of that classic song, and so we just had to do it. The record company was happy to have it because of *Hey Joe's* dodgy content."

The Vibrators drew on two distinct *Hey Joe* influences, the first being the driving guitar licks of Hendrix, no surprise there, and the second, with a nod to what Edwards saw as "the aggressiveness of the song," the long ago version by The Leaves.

"We put those two influences together when we

went into the studio. Our intent was to just go for it and do it live. We ended up recording *Hey Joe* in under an hour. If you're going to do a *Hey Joe*, you don't want to stop every five seconds trying to get everything absolutely right. Our intent with *Hey Joe* was not to have everything be perfect. We were trying to get the energy, the enthusiasm and the power of the song across. We didn't want to be playing the song 55 times. Ours was the all slam bam version."

Edwards claims that the result may well have been a shock to even the discerning hip UK punk listeners. "They were probably surprised at our version, and had not really heard anything like it before. That's why we did it."

At the end of the day, Edwards acknowledges that *Hey Joe's* perceived simplicity is only one reason why it remains a popular and much recorded song to this day. "Yeah it's simple, but it's also dangerous and powerful. You can make it as easy or difficult as you want. It's just a good song to play. It just works."

Bap Kennedy is one of those below-the-recognition-line country rock kind of guys. He's just slick enough and just raw enough, with a highly appealing sound and style, to get through the day and make a go of it. His cover of *Hey Joe,* which appeared on his 2009 album *Howl On,* is a solid amalgamation of all his strengths: a chugging, tangy guitar lead running a healthy race with a solid bottom sound and straightforward, slightly understated vocals. Bap's *Hey Joe* is a journeyman vision of the song, something just enticing enough to get the listener in a good mood until the next take comes along.

By the mid 2000's, sophistication was in the air

when it came to interpreting *Hey Joe*. It was not uncommon for non-rock musicians to replace *Hey Joe's* expected bombast and angst with lighter shades of subtlety and tone. As indicated previously, the jazz community had embraced the more introspective side of *Hey Joe* with a fervor. For them, the song had evolved into something deeper and more thought provoking. Typical of this jazz/bop/thinking man's movement was jazz pianist Brad Mehldau, who, on his 2012 album of cover tunes *What Do You Start*, showcased his *Hey Joe* as a mid- tempo piece with his staccato piano riffs and mid-song florid runs, into an interesting, and soulful, somewhat new twist on the *Hey Joe* tale.

2012 was also the year when another *Hey Joe* nugget, courtesy of the equally long lost Australian band Pond came out to play. *Pond's Hey Joe* was initially released sometime in 1965. The band, as well as the record, at least on American shores, would soon be wiped from the public consciousness, only to return in 2012 within the grooves of a monster compilation entitled *Nuggets: Antipodian Interpolaions of The First Psychedelic Era.* This take is a fairly easy one to critique. They sound exactly like The Leaves. Which, in turn, leads one to contemplate and reexamine just how good The Leaves actually were.

Charlotte Gainsbourg has long been an actress, but also became a singer willing to take a chance. In 2013 she took one giant step as an actress when she took on the porno art film *Nymphomaniac* that had emerged from the mind of its often-controversial director Lars Van Trier. As an afterthought to the controversial proceedings, Gainsbourg, aided and abetted by musician/producer Beck, came up with the idea of the actress turning singer on the project, to add a song to the film's soundtrack. That song would turn out to be *Hey Joe*.

To Gainsbourg's way of thinking, *Hey Joe* could be the ideal emotional counter to the psychological rigors of acting in *Nymphomaniac* and the subsequent *Nymphomaniac II*. Away from the script, and psychologically on her own, she would be free to examine and interpret her deepest feelings in the context of the equally dark song.

A version of the song that would easily contradict the idea of pigeonholing and predictability, in Gainbourg's and Beck's hands *Hey Joe* sounds vaguely familiar at first, but is finally something new and challenging. Gainsbourg's low, whispery vocals are alternately confessional and accusatory, quietly exploring the film's erotic conceit. The fragments and finely clipped instrumentation are precise, controlled and detailed in a very dark way. Ultimately, this version of *Hey Joe* radiates a 70's decadent vibe, a taut sense of sexual tension and danger amidst a tone of dark exploration and discovery. In other words, it's pretty damned good stuff.

Despite the nature of *Hey Joe*'s lyrics and the ultra- violent nature of the world today, *Hey Joe* and the real world had never remotely crossed paths until mid February 2013, when, shortly after a BBC news report of the ongoing murder trial of para-Olympian Oscar Pistorious, accused of shooting and killing his super model girlfriend, *BB6 Music*, in a brash bit of gallows humor, saw fit to follow the news item with a snippet of the song *Hey Joe*. The ghoulish nature of the transition was not lost on listeners, and the *BBC* was forced to beat a strategic retreat with numerous apologies and an official mea culpa from a *BBC* spokesperson. "In light of the nature of the news item, we apologize for any offence caused by the proximity of the song *Hey Joe* to the news bulletin," he said.

By association, *Hey Joe* was now Public Enemy Number One.

Chapter Seventeen

More *Joe* To Come

So you think that there is no more *Hey Joe* to be discovered and savored? End of story? On to the next obscurity? Guess again.

Hey Joe is still very much out there and thriving like all get out, closing in on an estimated 3000 recorded versions, if the latest count is to be believed. *Hey Joe* continues to make an indelible mark. At its core, it remains a simple song and a simple message: a primordial touchstone on the dark side of the human soul. Some 50 years since The Leaves, Hendrix and all the pretenders to the *Hey Joe* throne, the song is still as easy to play as when Billy Roberts, Tim Rose and others strummed those classic, primitive chords and told its story in simplicity and directness.

HeyJoeCovers.fr continues to dig deep. Updated on a regular basis, the dedicated website, run with passion by the enthusiastic and possessed Christian Arnould, continues to discover and report obscurities. In 2015 alone, easily a dozen recorded takes, everything from jazz, to solo acoustic, to rock and pop and back again were dutifully reported for the first time. Unknowns and obscurities seemed to be the bulk of this latest group of inductees into *Hey Joe* infamy. They include The Camaros, Dee Alexander, Erika Stucky, Joscho Stephan, Jussi Hamalaainen, Kastro, Kofo The Wonderman, Solo Razafindrakoto and The Stencils. There is even an album of all instrumental tracks including *Hey Joe* listed from an unknown artist called Tip Band.

On the same website, the collector-friendly sidebar of versions of *Hey Joe* that may or may not exist includes vague references to *Hey Joe* done by Alice Cooper, Tim Buckley, George Thorogood, Tom Waits, Jose Feliciano (a bit of a ghostly version reportedly heard only by listeners of the BBC) and Crowded House. The late blues great Jimmy Dawkins reportedly has a version on a 1994 live disc out there in the weeds called *Live Baltimore*, of which there is no official record. There's reportedly a live version by Ted Nugent that has defied detection. And in the irony of ironies, more than one hardcore collector has it on good authority that Chester Powers a/k/a Dino Valenti a/k/a the cat who claimed he wrote *Hey Joe* before John Law came in and busted his ass, has a concert recording of *Hey Joe* that may or may not exist, but if it does, it has him singing that gruff and gnarly version of *Hey Joe*.

If this doesn't get your *Hey Joe* Jones going...well you get the picture. Much like other examples of the *Hey Joe* experience, there's a mania for finding each and every nugget, and the one thing diehard *Hey Joe* fanatics can be secure in is the idea that there is always somebody out there recording a version of *Hey Joe,* and whether it truly exists or not...

...They've gotta have it.

Which means this book will never be truly complete, and my work will never truly be done.

Hey Joe has become a lightning rod for countless musicians. It's simplicity has been a guardian at the gates, standing stark in its directness, daring anyone to take a shot and see if they can do better.

Over the course of 50-plus years, *Hey Joe* has morphed into something far larger than a mere throwaway pop song. It's become a universal symbol of everything that is defiant in a complacent world. *Hey Joe* is everything we want to be: angry, dangerous and, by degrees, over the top in its daring insistence on going to the dark side. It is a voyage of constant discovery that will continue to be taken far into the future.

There will always be *Hey Joe.* A future without this song would be a blow to whatever drives us to dangerous and exciting ground. *Hey Joe i*s a runaway train that is constantly leaving the station for parts unknown. Hear those wheels screeching down the tracks and into an uncertain night?

If you listen closely you'll swear they're whispering, "Hey Joe where you going with that gun in your hand?"

APPENDIX

HEY JOE SOUNDTRACK CONTRIBUTIONS

Over the years, *Hey Joe* had become a go-to song for films, television and documentaries. Not surprisingly, Hendrix's version, either as a snippet or the full song, made the biggest splash in various cinematic media. But as you will discover, other takes on the classic *Hey Joe* made appearances as well.

JIMI HENDRIX...*HEY JOE*

MOTION PICTURES

Forest Gump, Empire Records, Wayne's World 2, Death Sentence, Reaper, Harold & Kumar Escape From Guantanamo Bay, Crooklyn, The Wild Life, Panther.

DOCUMENTARIES

Jimi Plays Monterey, Jimi Hendrix: Live At Woodstock, Jimi Hendrix: The Guitar Hero.

TELEVISION

Star Trek: Deep Space Nine, The King of Queens, Rage, 60/90, My Mad Fat Diary

NON-HENDRIX SOUNDTRACK CONTRIBUTIONS

Actor Michael Pitt with the band Twins of Evil in the film *The Dreamers*.

Pink Floyd's Roger Waters, in the song *Folded Flags* in the film soundtrack *When The Wind Blows*, references *Hey Joe* in the lines 'Hey Joe where you going with that gun in your hands,' and 'Hey Joe, where you going with that dogma in your head.'

Linkin Park's Mike Shinoda sampled Hendrix's version of his own *Jimi Remix of the Styles of Beyond* song *Bleach* which appeared on their *Fort Minor We Major* mixtape.

Rapper Fat Joe used the line "Hey Joe, where you going with that gun in your hand" in the song *Joey Don't Do It* from the album *Jealous One Still Envy 2*.

SOURCES

INTERVIEWS

A wide variety of musicians, producers, fellow authors and other people involved behind the scenes in all things *Hey Joe* provided their time and memories. They include Keith Olsen, Rob Landes, Don Preston, Maxwell Pickett, Toody Cole, Randy Holden, John 'Eddie' Edwards, John Medeski, Vernon Reid, Otis Taylor, Philippe Rault, Ted Fox, Jerry Hopkins, Bo Goldsen, Mike Rivers, Dave Hull.

A VERY SPECIAL THANKS TO...

Authors John Einarson and Bruno Ceriotta, the authors of two excellent books whose detailed odysseys crossed paths with *Hey Joe*, and were generous enough to offer me the bits and pieces of their research that pertained to *Hey Joe* that expanded my search in the best possible way. Consider your books officially plugged.

BOOKS

The Guinness Book of World Records (1955-Present), *Ozark Folksongs Vol. II* (1948), *The Jimi Hendrix Experience* by Jerry Hopkins (Arcade Publishing 2014), *Mr. Tambourine Man: The Life and Legacy of The Byrds' Gene Clark* by John Einarson (Backbeat Books

2005), *The Byrds: Timeless Flight* by Johnny Rogan (Scorpion Publications 1980), *60's Rock: Garage Psychedelic and Other Satisfactions* by Michael Hicks (University Of Illinois Press 1999), *My Little Red Book: Love Day By Day 1945-1971* by Bruno Ceriotti (Soundcheck Books 2016), *The Ultimate Hendrix: An Illustrated Encyclopedia of Live Concerts and Sessions* by John McDermott, Eddie Kramer and Billy Cox (Hal Leonard Corporation 2009), *The Complete Book of British Charts* by Tony Brown, Jon Kutner and Neil Warwick (Omnibus Press 2000), *Tangled Up In Tapes: A Recording History of Bob Dylan* by Glen Dundas (SMA Services 1999). *The Words and Music of Jimi Hendrix* by David V. Moskowitz (Pragur 2010), *The California Sound: An Insiders Story* by Stephen McParland, *Which Side Are You On: An Inside History Of The Folk Music Revival In America* by Dick Weissman (Bloombury Academic 2006)

WEBSITES

HeyJoeVersions.com, *HeyJoeCovers.fr*,
RockCellarMagazine.com, *Guitarworld.com*,
Popsickle.com, *TheByrdsLyricPage.com*,
60sGarageBands.com, *OpulentConceptions.com*,
StraightAhead.com, *TheHendrixGuide.com*,
Songfacts.com, *WilsonPickett.com*,
UnderTheRadar.com, *MonstersandCritics.com*, *Axi
Entertainment.com*, *AisEntertainment.com*,
TimRoseTheMusician.com,
Ontheflipside.blogspot.com, *Rockandrollarchives.com*.
PerfectSoundForever.com, *Ptolemaic Terrascape.com*.

MAGAZINES
Rolling Stone, No Depression, Ugly Things, Canal Magazine.

NEWSPAPERS
The Independent, New Music Express, The Guardian, The Observer, Daily Express

TELEVISION AND RADIO
Later...With Joolz Holland, The Howard Stern Show

MISCELLANEOUS
Album liner notes for *Jimi Hendrix: The Ultimate Experience, Decca Records release schedule, interview by Richie Unterberger, Acoustic Guitar Videos, Jas Obrecht article*, Liner notes for *See The Rain: The CBS Years 2003, The Library Of Congress.*

About the Author

New York Times bestselling author Marc Shapiro has written more than 60 nonfiction celebrity biographies, more than two-dozen comic books, numerous short stories and poetry, and three short form screenplays. He is also a veteran freelance entertainment journalist.

His young adult book *JK Rowling: The Wizard Behind Harry Potter* was on *The New York Times* bestseller list for four straight weeks. His fact-based book *Total Titanic* was also on *The Los Angeles Times* bestseller list for four weeks. *Justin Bieber: The Fever* was on the nationwide Canadian bestseller list for several weeks.

Shapiro has written books on such personalities as Shonda Rhimes, George Harrison, Carlos Santana, Annette Funicello, Lorde, Lindsay Johan, E.L. James, Jamie Dornan, Dakota Johnson, Adele and countless others. He also co-authored the autobiography of mixed martial arts fighter Tito Ortiz, *This Is Gonna Hurt: The Life of a Mixed Martial Arts Champion.*

He is currently working on a book on the Canadian rock band, Tragically Hip, as well as updating his biographies of Gillian Anderson and Lucy Lawless for Riverdale Avenue Books.

Other Riverdale Avenue Books Titles by Marc Shapiro

Trump This! The Life and Times of Donald Trump, An Unauthorized Biography

The Secret Life of EL James

The Real Steele: The Unauthorized Biography of Dakota Johnson

Inside Grey's Anatomy: The Unauthorized Biography of Jamie Dornan

Annette Funicello: America's Sweetheart

Game: The Resurrection of Tim Tebow

Legally Bieber: Justin Bieber at 18

Lindsay Lohan: Fully Loaded, From Disney to Disaster

Lorde: Your Heroine, How This Young Feminist Broke the Rules and Succeeded

We Love Jenni: An Unauthorized Biography

Who Is Katie Holmes? An Unauthorized Biography

*Norman Reedus: True Tales of The Waking Dead's
Zombie Hunter,
An Unauthorized Biography*

*Welcome to Shondaland: An Unauthorized Biography
of Shonda Rhimes*

www.ingramcontent.com/pod-product-compliance
Lightning Source LLC
Chambersburg PA
CBHW072008090426
42740CB00011B/2142